1991 SUPPLEMENT

TO

THE FIRST AMENDMENT AND THE FIFTH ESTATE
REGULATION OF ELECTRONIC MASS MEDIA

BY

T. BARTON CARTER
Associate Professor of Mass Communication
College of Communication
Boston University

MARC A. FRANKLIN
Frederick I. Richman Professor of Law
Stanford University

and

JAY B. WRIGHT
Professor of Journalism
S. I. Newhouse School of Public Communications
Syracuse University

Westbury, New York
The Foundation Press, Inc.
1991

TABLE OF CONTENTS

CHAPTER V

CHAPTER VIII

There are no additions to Chapter VIII.

CHAPTER IX

CHAPTER XIII

CHAPTER XIV

Chapter I

INTRODUCTION

Add to casebook p. 22, after 2nd full paragraph:

Protection for symbolic speech stirred public opinion in June 1989 when the Supreme Court decided 5-4 that a Texas flag-desecration law was unconstitutional because of the First Amendment. Texas v. Johnson, 109 S.Ct. 2533 (1989). The decision led to widespread calls for a Constitutional amendment and to the Federal Flag Protection Act of 1989, Congress's own attempt to protect the American flag from being burned or defaced. In two cases decided a year later, the Court, with the same 5-4 split, found the federal statute constitutionally flawed in the same way as the Texas statute because it suppressed expression. United States v. Eichman and United States v. Haggerty, 110 S.Ct. 2404 (1990). Public opinion polls made clear that the First Amendment is not always popular; a New York Times/CBS News poll that year found that 83 percent of respondents thought flag burning should be against the law, and 59 percent would favor a constitutional amendment if it were the only way to make flag destruction illegal. New York Times, June 12, 1990, at p. B7. Critics said that making such an exception to the First Amendment would set a dangerous precedent.

Add to casebook p. 27, after last full paragraph:

A publisher was enjoined in August 1989 from publishing *Spy Notes*, a book created by *Spy* magazine to look and feel like *Cliff's Notes* study guides with their trademarked yellow and black diagonal striped design. The action sought trademark protection under the Lanham Act. A federal district court rejected the assertion that *Spy Notes* was merely a parody and found a "profound" likelihood of confusion between the study guides and *Spy Notes*. Cliff's Notes, Inc. v. Bantam Doubleday Dell Publishing Group Inc., 718 F.Supp.1159, 16 Med.L.Rptr. 2025 (S.D.N.Y.1989). The U.S. Court of Appeals for the Second Circuit vacated the injunction a month later, holding that the public interest in free expression must be weighed against public interest in avoiding consumer confusion. The court thought *Spy Notes* was a parody and that the risk of confusion was slight. Cliff's Notes, Inc. v. Bantam Doubleday Dell Publishing Group inc., 886 F.2d 490, 16 Med.L.Rptr. 2289 (2d Cir.1989).

Several restraints were imposed in 1990, but all were short-lived. The syndicated news program "Inside Edition" was temporarily restrained in January 1990 from broadcasting a videotape of a physician allegedly engaged in malpractice. The doctor claimed that "Inside Edition" had violated a statute prohibiting interception and disclosure of wire communications or oral communications (18 U.S.C.A. § 2511). The order was vacated 11 days later by the court of appeals, which held that § 2511 "in no way provides for a prior restraint of the press in their exercise of first amendment rights, even if the press's conduct clearly violates" the section. In re King World Productions Inc., 898 F.2d 56, 17 Med.L.Rptr. 1531 (1990).

Lifetime Cable was briefly subjected to an order restraining it from showing "Hilary in Hiding," a British Broadcasting Corp. film about the battle between Eric Foretich and Elizabeth Morgan over custody of their child. The order was issued April 6, 1990, after the father said irreparable harm would come to the child if the scenes of her describing alleged sexual abuse were shown. It was vacated the same day by the U.S. Court of Appeals for the District of Columbia. The latter held that any rights the father and child have must be redressed in legal actions "that do not require a prior restraint in derogation of the First Amendment." In re Lifetime Cable, 17 Med.L.Rptr. 1648 (1990). See also Broadcasting, April 16, 1990, at 73.

In another case, the government of Israel tried to stop distribution of Victor Ostrovsky's book, *By Way of Deception: A Devastating Insider's Portrait of the Mossad.* Faced with the argument that Israeli intelligence agents would be killed if the book were distributed, a judge in New York temporarily restrained publication, but the order was overturned the next day. The book had been restrained in Canada, but approximately 1,500 wholesalers and book reviewers had already received copies of the book, and 17,000 books had already been shipped to stores. State of

Israel v. St. Martin's Press, Inc., 560 N.Y.S.2d 450 (App.Div. 1st Dept.1990).

In remarks at a communications law seminar in November 1990, prominent attorney Floyd Abrams remarked that "[t]he near-total ban on prior restraints we used to talk about seems secure but in a rather insecure way," noting the several prior restraint attempts during the year." "The reasons for prior restraint *always* sound pretty good," Abrams said, "and the potential for damage to First Amendment rights *always* sounds minimal, yet appellate courts have reversed consistently and quickly."

That same month the issue of a prior restraint to protect a defendant's fair trial rights arose again in the case of former Panamanian leader Manuel Noriega, and it was not so quickly released. Cable News Network (CNN) had obtained tape recordings of Noriega talking to members of his defense team. Normally, of course, attorney-client conversations are confidential. Fearing that Noriega's future trial could be prejudiced by CNN's playing of the tapes, the U.S. District Court for the Southern District of Florida issued a temporary restraining order barring their playing. The U.S. Court of Appeals for the Eleventh Circuit affirmed the ruling, and the Supreme Court, without a written opinion, refused to overrule the lower courts or to review the order. Cable News Network v. Noriega, 111 S.Ct. 451, 18 Med.L.Rptr. 1358 (1990). Justices Thurgood Marshall and Sandra Day O'Connor dissented. The Supreme Court's action would not necessarily have precluded their considering the prior restraint later, but the trial court subsequently lifted the restraint and essentially ended the dispute.

Chapter II

THE SPECTRUM AND ITS UTILIZATION

Add to casebook p. 47, after 1st paragraph:

As of July 1991, the FCC had failed to make final decisions on how to allot the new band. The decision is now expected in late 1991 with licensing for the new stations to begin in late 1992.

Add to casebook p. 54, after 4th full paragraph:

In September 1990 the Commission announced that it intends to select a simulcast HDTV system. No further consideration will be given to augmentation systems. Although the Commission did not envision selecting an EDTV system prior to the selection of an HDTV system, it left open the possibility that such a system could be selected at some time in the future.

The FCC gave several reasons for the rejection of augmentation systems in favor of simulcast. First, simulcast systems, able to use all new technology, "offer the potential for significantly greater improvement in the quality of television picture and audio performance" than augmentation systems, which have to incorporated the now antiquated NTSC technology.

A simulcast system also will be spectrum efficient and facilitate the implementation of ATV service. Such a system will transmit the increased information of an HDTV signal in the same 6 Mhz channel space used in the current television channel plan. This ultimately will minimize the amount of spectrum needed for HDTV service and simplify the HDTV channel allocation process. . . . In addition, a simulcast system will provide consumers with the greatest degree of initial improvement in the quality of television picture and audio service. Finally, our selection of a simulcast system will eliminate confusion for consumers about which

type of receiver to purchase.   This latter
factor can be expected to speed the growth of
HDTV receiver penetration.

The Commission also noted that existing spectrum
restrictions would force many stations to transmit
their primary signal in the VHF band and their
augmentation channel in the UHF band. Because signals
in these two bands have different propagation
characteristics, there would be additional technical
problems for augmentation systems resulting in more
expensive receivers. Advanced Television Systems, 68
R.R.2d 167 (1990).

Chapter III

JUSTIFICATIONS FOR GOVERNMENT REGULATION

There are no additions to Chapter III.

Chapter IV

BROADCAST LICENSING

Add to casebook p. 96, after 2nd full paragraph:

The policy statement was upheld on appeal. National Association for Better Broadcasting v. Federal Communications Commission, 830 F.2d 270, (D.C.Cir.1987).

Several years later the Commission expanded the scope of character examinations to include any felony conviction, regardless of whether it was broadcast related or not. The FCC's rationale for this expansion was that "[b]ecause all felonies are serious crimes, any conviction provides an indication of an applicant's or licensee's propensity to obey the law." The FCC also expanded consideration of antitrust violations to cover all mass-media-related violations instead of just broadcast-related ones.

With regard to both felony convictions and antitrust violations the Commission will, however, continue to take into consideration mitigating factors such as "the willfulness of the misconduct, the frequency of the misconduct, the currentness of the misconduct, the seriousness of the misconduct, the nature of the participation (if any) of managers or owners, efforts made to remedy the wrong, overall record of compliance with FCC rules and policies, and rehabilitation." The Commission also reiterated its willingness to condition license grants on the outcome of allegations being adjudicated in courts or other agencies. Character Qualifications Policy, 5 F.C.C.Rcd. 3252, 67 R.R.2d 1107 (1990).

On reconsideration, the FCC clarified its position with regard to misdemeanor convictions. They do not have to be reported to the Commission, but in appropriate cases serious misdemeanor convictions may be considered in evaluating the character qualifications of an applicant. Character Qualifications Policy, 69 R.R.2d 279 (1991).

Add to casebook p. 110, after note 3:

4. As part of a continuing effort to cut down on such abuses as filing sham applications for the sole purpose of extracting money from legitimate applicants in return for withdrawal of the application, the Commission imposed new limitations on settlement payments in comparative proceedings for new broadcast stations.   Settlement payments are limited to legitimate and prudent out-of-pocket expenses. Comparative Broadcast Hearings (Settlement Agreement Payments), 68 R.R.2d 960 (1990).

Initially, even payments for legitimate and prudent expenses were to be permitted only until the trial phase of the hearing. From that point on, no settlement payments of any kind were to be permitted. However, on reconsideration, the Commission concluded that the legitimate-and-prudent-expenses limitation was sufficient to deter sham applications and that prohibiting any settlement payments after the start of a trial would only serve to deter parties from settling.   This result would be contrary to the primary purpose of new station proceedings, that of facilitating the expeditious delivery of new service to the public. Therefore, settlement payments for legitimate and prudent expenses will be permitted at any point of new broadcast station proceedings. Comparative Broadcast Hearings (Settlement Agreement Payments), 69 R.R.2d 175 (1991).

Add to casebook p. 113, after 3rd full paragraph:

Responding to the Commission's repeated requests for the authority to levy heavier forfeitures, Congress amended § 503(b)(2) in late 1989. Broadcasters and cable operators may now be assessed forfeitures of $25,000 per violation for each day of a continuing violation up to a maximum of $250,000 for any single act or failure to act. The Commission quickly adopted the new higher limits. Forfeitures, 67 R.R.2d 1193 (1990).

Add to casebook p. 115, after 3rd full paragraph:

In response to the Anti-Drug Abuse Act of 1988, the Commission announced a new ground for possible non-renewal or revocation. "[A]bsent extenuating or mitigating circumstances, the Commission intends promptly to take all appropriate steps, including initiation of license revocation proceedings, where information comes to our attention that FCC licensees or their principals have been convicted of drug trafficking." Drug Trafficking Policy, 66 R.R.2d 1617 (1989).

Add to casebook p. 133, after 1st paragraph:

In March 1990 the FCC took some initial steps towards curbing abuse of the license renewal process. First, the Commission adopted a prohibition on "all payments to competing applicants (other than the incumbent licensee) for the withdrawal of an application prior to the Initial Decision stage of a comparative hearing. Thereafter, we will approve settlements that do not exceed the withdrawing party's legitimate and prudent expenses for filing and litigating the competing application."

The Commission reasoned that this would weed out weak applications filed for the purpose of extracting settlement payments. The cost of staying in until an initial decision would be too great for a non *bona fide* applicant. Further, an applicant that lost in the initial decision stage would have very little leverage, especially if the initial decision was in the incumbent's favor.

At the same time allowing recovery of legitimate and prudent expenses after the initial decision provides "an efficient way to resolve comparative licensing proceedings, preserve funds for service to the public, and allow us to conserve our limited administrative resources."

The Commission also placed a legitimate and prudent expense limitation on settlements of petitions to deny:

41. We believe that a legitimate and
prudent expense limitation on settlement
payments of petitions to deny strikes the
appropriate balance between deterring abuse and
not discouraging the filing of such petitions.
By prohibiting payments in excess of legitimate
and prudent expenses we are removing the profit
motive for filing petitions to deny. This
should help ensure that petitions are filed for
legitimate public interest purposes. By
permitting recovery of legitimate and prudent
expenses, we are preserving the petition to deny
process as a monitoring and regulatory tool. It
is more likely that individuals or public
interest groups will perform their function of
informing us of licensee deficiencies if they
can maintain hope of recovery of the expenses
they incur. To preserve the private attorney
general function of petitions to deny, we
believe we should provide for the possibility
that a petitioner can be made economically
whole.

The FCC also announced that it would review all
future citizens' agreements--contracts in which
licensees agree to "implement a nonfinancial reform
such as a programming or an employment initiative" in
return for the dismissal of a petition to deny. In
determining whether an agreement furthers the public
interest the Commission:

. . . will presume that any agreement with a
petitioner that calls for the *petitioner*, or any
person or organization related to the
petitioner, to carry out for a fee, any
programming, employment or other "nonfinancial"
initiative does not further the public interest
and hence will be disapproved. As discussed
above, this type of arrangement is particularly
susceptible to abuse. In contrast, a licensee's
agreement with a petitioner to make changes in
operations or programming, either *by itself* or
through *disinterested third parties* without
further participation by the petitioner, will
likely be approved. For example, we will regard
an agreement to increase minority employment by
using, for a fee, the services of *petitioner* or
any person or organization related to

petitioner, as presumptively contrary to the public interest, and it will likely be disapproved. In contrast, we will regard an agreement to increase the pool of minority applicants for employment by contracting with a third party, completely independent from petitioner, as consistent with the public interest, and it will likely be approved.

The Commission will allow these presumptions to be rebutted by clear and convincing evidence that they are incorrect as applied to a specific citizens' agreement. Broadcast Renewal Applicants (Abuses of Comparative Renewal Process), 66 R.R.2d 708 (1989).

Various petitions for reconsideration were denied, 67 R.R.2d 1515 (1990). At the same time, the Commission adopted similar rules governing petitions to deny and citizens' agreements for new stations, license modification, and transfer applications. Abuses of the Broadcast Licensing and Allotment Processes, 67 R.R.2d 1526 (1990).

Add to casebook p. 133, after note 4:

The Commission upheld the Review Board's action and awarded Video 44 a renewal expectancy. The FCC argued that it should not give too much weight to the drop in non-entertainment programming at the end of the license term because that drop resulted in large part from Video 44's "experimentation" with an STV format. Video 44, 4 F.C.C.Rcd. 1209, 65 R.R.2d 1512 (1989).

The court of appeals reversed the renewal expectancy award as arbitrary and capricious. The court quoted its opinion in *Central Florida II* that the primary argument for renewal expectancy is that "the incumbent's past performance is some evidence, and perhaps the best evidence, of what its future performance would be." Given that there was no evidence that the switch to STV was temporary, the station's performance under that format was better evidence than its performance under a previous format of what its future service to the public would be. The court remanded the case to the Commission "with instructions to focus on the downward trend in Video

44's non-entertainment programming through the latter stages of the previous license period in order to predict Video 44's likely performance in the license period at issue here." Monroe Communications Corp. v. Federal Communications Commission, 900 F.2d 351, 67 R.R.2d 843 (D.C.Cir.1990).

On remand, the Commission found that Video 44's late term performance did not justify any renewal expectancy. With the elimination of Video 44's renewal expectancy preference, Monroe's preferences for integration and diversity became controlling. Video 44, 68 R.R.2d 503 (1990).

Add to casebook p. 151, after note 1:

1a.   In *Character Qualifications in Broadcast Licensing*, p. 96 (the casebook), *supra*, the Commission adopted a rule prohibiting applicants and licensees from making any written "misrepresentation or willful material omission[s] bearing on any matter within the jurisdiction of the Commission." 47 C.F.R. § 73.1015. In *Character Qualifications Policy*, p. ??? (this supplement), *supra*, the FCC amended Part I of its rules in order to emphasize that this requirement applies to all FCC applicants, licensees and permittees, not just those involved in broadcasting. 47 C.F.R. § 1.17.

Add to casebook p. 153, after last full paragraph:

A settlement agreement for the last of the RKO stations was approved in early 1991. The terms were similar to the other RKO settlement agreements with RKO receiving significantly less than 75 percent of the station's fair market value. RKO General, Inc. (KFRC), 68 R.R.2d 1341 (1991).

Chapter V

MEDIA CONCENTRATION

Add to casebook p. 158, after 4th full paragraph:

Soon after the modifications in the duopoly rule were announced, the Commission ruled on the waiver request of Capital Cities/ABC, whose merger, p. 177 (the casebook), *infra*, had produced ownership of TV-AM-FM combinations in New York City, Chicago, and Los Angeles and of an AM-FM combination in San Francisco. It granted permanent waivers in all four cases because all four cities were in the top 25 television markets and each had over 30 separately owned and operated broadcast stations after the proposed waivers. The FCC found 94 separate licensees in New York, 105 in Chicago, 79 in Los Angeles and 57 in San Francisco. The Commission did not scrutinize each proposal for economic efficiencies because it had already concluded that such efficiencies generally exist. Allowing the combinations would not undermine the benefits that flow from the "Commission's traditional pro-competitive and diversity policies."

Commissioner Dennis concurred separately. She had suggested a two-tier approach in lieu of the 25 market-30 licensee approach. She would have restricted waivers to markets with at least 10 television stations, 45 separate owners and 65 broadcast stations. "In all other markets, we should not only retain the rule, but enforce it strictly." Because the four markets involved here met even her tighter requirements, she concurred. Capital Cities/ABC, Inc., 66 R.R.2d 1146 (1989).

Add to casebook p. 185, replacing note 6:

METRO BROADCASTING, INC. v. FEDERAL COMMUNICATIONS COMMISSION

Supreme Court of the United States, 1990.
110 S.Ct. 2997, 67 R.R.2d 1353.

JUSTICE BRENNAN delivered the opinion of the Court.

The issue in these cases, consolidated for decision today, is whether certain minority preference policies of the Federal Communications Commission violate the equal protection component of the Fifth Amendment. The policies in question are (1) a program awarding an enhancement for minority ownership in comparative proceedings for new licenses, and (2) the minority "distress sale" program, which permits a limited category of existing radio and television broadcast stations to be transferred only to minority-controlled firms. We hold that these policies do not violate equal protection principles.

I

A

The policies before us today can best be understood by reference to the history of federal efforts to promote minority participation in the broadcast industry.[1] . . . Although for the past two decades minorities have constituted at least one-fifth of the United States population, during this time relatively few members of minority groups have held broadcast licenses. In 1971, minorities owned only 10 of the approximately 7,500 radio stations in the country and none of the more than 1,000 television stations, [ ]; in 1978, minorities owned less than 1 percent of the Nation's radio and television stations, [ ]; and in 1986, they owned just 2.1 percent of the more than 11,000 radio and television stations in the

---

1. The FCC has defined the term "minority" to include "those of Black, Hispanic Surnamed, American Eskimo, Aleut, American Indian and Asiatic American extraction." Statement of Policy on Minority Ownership of Broadcasting Facilities, 68 F.C.C.2d 979, 980, n. 8 (1978). . . .

United States. [ ] . . . Moreover, these statistics fail to reflect the fact that, as late entrants who often have been able to obtain only the less valuable stations, many minority broadcasters serve geographically limited markets with relatively small audiences.

The Commission has recognized that the viewing and listening public suffers when minorities are underrepresented among owners of television and radio stations:

> "Acute underrepresentation of minorities among the owners of broadcast properties is troublesome because it is the licensee who is ultimately responsible for identifying and serving the needs and interests of his or her audience. Unless minorities are encouraged to enter the mainstream of the commercial broadcasting business, a substantial portion of our citizenry will remain underserved and the larger, non-minority audience will be deprived of the views of minorities." [ ]

The Commission has therefore worked to encourage minority participation in the broadcast industry. The FCC began by formulating rules to prohibit licensees from discriminating against minorities in employment. The FCC explained that "broadcasting is an important mass media form which, because it makes use of the airwaves belonging to the public, must obtain a federal license under a public interest standard and must operate in the public interest in order to obtain periodic renewals of that license." [ ] Regulations dealing with employment practices were justified as necessary to enable the FCC to satisfy its obligation under the Communications Act to promote diversity of programming. [ ] The United States Department of Justice, for example, contended that equal employment opportunity in the broadcast industry could "'contribute significantly toward reducing and ending discrimination in other industries'" because of the "'enormous impact which television and radio have upon American life.'" [ ]

Initially, the FCC did not consider minority status as a factor in licensing decisions, maintaining as a matter of Commission policy that no preference to

minority ownership was warranted where the record in
a particular case did not give assurances that the
owner's race likely would affect the content of the
station's broadcast service to the public. [ ] [This
position was overruled in *TV 9*, p. 105 (the casebook),
supra.]

    . . .   [T]he FCC adopted in May 1978 its
*Statement of Policy on Minority Ownership of
Broadcasting Facilities*, 68 F.C.C.2d 979.   After
recounting its past efforts to expand broadcast
diversity, the FCC concluded:

> "[W]e are compelled to observe that the views of
> racial minorities continue to be inadequately
> represented in the broadcast media.   This
> situation is detrimental not only to the
> minority audience but to all of the viewing and
> listening public.   Adequate representation of
> minority viewpoints in programming serves not
> only the needs and interests of the minority
> community but also enriches and educates the
> non-minority audience.   It enhances the
> diversified programming which is a key objective
> not only of the Communications Act of 1934 but
> also of the First Amendment."   [ ]

Describing its actions as only "first steps," [ ], the
FCC outlined two elements of a minority ownership
policy.

    First,   the Commission pledged to consider
minority ownership as one factor in comparative
proceedings for new licenses.   [Here, the Court
outlined the six comparative criteria used for
mutually exclusive license applications, p. 99-102
(the casebook), *supra*.] In the Policy Statement on
Minority Ownership, the FCC announced that minority
ownership and participation in management would be
considered as a "plus" to be weighed together with all
other relevant factors.   [ ] The "plus" is awarded
only to the extent that a minority owner actively
participates in the day-to-day management of the
station.

    Second, the FCC outlined a plan to increase
minority opportunities to receive reassigned and
transferred licenses through the so-called "distress

sale" policy. [ ] As a general rule, a licensee whose qualifications to hold a broadcast license come into question may not assign or transfer the license until the FCC has resolved its doubts in a noncomparative hearing. The distress sale policy is an exception to that practice, allowing a broadcaster whose license has been designated for a revocation hearing, to assign the license to an FCC-approved minority enterprise. [ ] The assignee must meet the FCC's basic qualifications, and the minority ownership must exceed 50 percent or be controlling.[6] The buyer must purchase the license before the start of the revocation or renewal hearing, and the price must not exceed 75 percent of fair market value. These two Commission minority ownership policies are at issue today.

B

1

. . . [P]etitioner Metro Broadcasting, Inc. (Metro) challenges the Commission's policy awarding preferences to minority owners in comparative licensing proceedings. Several applicants, including Metro and Rainbow Broadcasting (Rainbow), were involved in a comparative proceeding to select among three mutually exclusive proposals to construct and operate a new UHF television station in the Orlando, Florida, metropolitan area. . . . [The Commission's Review Board considered] Rainbow's comparative showing and found it superior to Metro's. In so doing, the Review Board awarded Rainbow a substantial enhancement on the ground that it was 90 percent Hispanic-owned, whereas Metro had only one minority partner who owned 19.8 percent of the enterprise. The Review Board found that Rainbow's minority credit outweighed Metro's local residence and civic participation advantage. [ ] The Commission denied review of the Board's decision largely without discussion, stating

---

6. In 1982, the FCC determined that a limited partnership could qualify as a minority enterprise if the general partner is a minority who holds at least 20 percent interest and who will exercise "complete control over a station's affairs." [ ]

merely that it "agree[d] with the Board's resolution
of this case."   [ ]

    [The court of appeals affirmed the decision, 2-1,
and petitions for rehearing were denied.]

                          2

    [The other case] emerged from a series of
attempts by Faith Center, Inc., the licensee of a
Hartford, Connecticut television station, to execute
a minority distress sale. In December 1980, the FCC
designated for a hearing Faith Center's application
for renewal of its license.   [ ]   [Faith Center
obtained FCC approval for a distress sale, but the
sale fell through due to financing problems. A second
attempt at a distress sale was approved, this time
over the objections of Alan Shurberg. The second sale
also fell through due to financing problems.]

    In   December   1983,   respondent   Shurberg
Broadcasting of Hartford, Inc. (Shurberg) applied to
the Commission for a permit to build a television
station in Hartford. The application was mutually
exclusive with Faith Center's renewal application,
then still pending. In June 1984, Faith Center again
sought the FCC's approval for a distress sale,
requesting permission to sell the station to Astroline
Communications   Company,   Limited   Partnership
(Astroline), a minority applicant. Shurberg opposed
the sale to Astroline on a number of grounds,
including that the FCC's distress sale program
violated Shurberg's right to equal protection.
Shurberg therefore urged the Commission to deny the
distress sale request and to schedule a comparative
hearing to examine the application Shurberg had
tendered alongside Faith Center's renewal request. In
December 1984, the FCC approved Faith Center's
petition for permission to assign its broadcast
license to Astroline pursuant to the distress sale
policy.   [ ]   The FCC rejected Shurberg's equal
protection challenge to the policy as "without merit."
[ ]

    [The court of appeals, 2-1, held that the
distress sale policy was unconstitutional. The
majority found that the policy "unconstitutionally
deprives Alan Shurberg and Shurberg Broadcasting of

their equal protection rights under the Fifth
Amendment because the program is not narrowly tailored
to remedy past discrimination or to promote
programming diversity."]

II

It is of overriding significance in these cases
that the FCC's minority ownership programs have been
specifically approved--indeed mandated--by Congress.
. . .

. . . We hold that benign race-conscious
measures mandated by Congress--even if those measures
are not "remedial" in the sense of being designed to
compensate victims of past governmental or societal
discrimination--are constitutionally permissible to
the extent that they serve important governmental
objectives within the power of Congress and are
substantially related to achievement of those
objectives.

. . .

We hold that the FCC minority ownership policies
pass muster under the test we announce today. First
we find that they serve the important governmental
objective of broadcast diversity. Second, we conclude
that they are substantially related to the achievement
of hat objective.

A

Congress found that "the effects of past
inequities stemming from racial and ethnic
discrimination have resulted in a severe
underrepresentation of minorities in the media of mass
communications." [ ] Congress and the Commission do
not justify the minority ownership policies strictly
as remedies for victims of this discrimination,
however. Rather, Congress and the FCC have selected
the minority ownership policies primarily to promote
programming diversity, and they urge that such
diversity is an important governmental objective that
can serve as a constitutional basis for the preference
policies. We agree.

We have long recognized that "[b]ecause of the scarcity of [electromagnetic] frequencies, the Government is permitted to put restraints on licensees in favor of others whose views should be expressed on this unique medium." [*Red Lion*] The Government's role in distributing the limited number of broadcast licenses is not merely that of a "traffic officer," [*NBC*]; rather it is axiomatic that broadcasting may be regulated in light of the rights of the viewing and listening audience and that "the widest possible dissemination of information from diverse and antagonistic sources is essential to the welfare of the public." [*AP*] Safeguarding the public's right to receive a diversity of views and information over the airwaves is therefore an integral component of the FCC's mission. We have observed that "'the "public interest" standard necessarily invites reference to First Amendment principles,'" [*NCCB*], and that the Communications Act has designated broadcasters as "fiduciaries for the public." [*League of Women Voters*]. "[T]he people as a whole retain their interest in free speech by radio [and other forms of broadcast] and their collective right to have the medium function consistently with the ends and purposes of the First Amendment," and "[i]t is the right of the viewers and listeners, not the right of the broadcasters, which is paramount." [*Red Lion*] "Congress may . . . seek to assure that the public receives through this medium a balanced presentation of information on issues of public importance that otherwise might not be addressed if control of the medium were left entirely in the hands of those who own and operate broadcasting stations." [*League of Women Voters*]

Against this background, we conclude that the interest in enhancing broadcast diversity is, at the very least, an important governmental objective and is therefore a sufficient basis for the Commission's minority ownership policies. . . . The benefits of such diversity are not limited to the members of minority groups who gain access to the broadcasting industry by virtue of the ownership policies; rather, the benefits redound to all members of the viewing and listening audience. . . .

B

We also find that the minority ownership policies are substantially related to the achievement of the Government's interest. One component of this inquiry concerns the relationship between expanded minority ownership and greater broadcast diversity; both the FCC and Congress have determined that such a relationship exists. Although we do not "'defer' to the judgment of the Congress and the Commission on a constitutional question," and would not "hesitate to invoke the Constitution should we determine that the Commission has not fulfilled its task with appropriate sensitivity" to equal protection principles, [*CBS v. DNC*], we must pay close attention to the expertise of the Commission and the factfinding of Congress when analyzing the nexus between minority ownership and programming diversity. With respect to this "complex" empirical question, *ibid*, we are required to give "great weight to the decisions of Congress and the experience of the Commission." *Id*, at 102.

1

. . .

Furthermore, the FCC's reasoning with respect to the minority ownership policies is consistent with longstanding practice under the Communications Act. From its inception, public regulation of broadcasting has been premised on the assumption that diversification of ownership will broaden the range of programming available to the broadcast audience. . . . The Commission has never relied on the market alone to ensure that the needs of the audience are met. Indeed, one of the FCC's elementary regulatory assumptions is that broadcast content is not purely market-driven; if it were, there would be little need for consideration in licensing decisions of such factors as integration of ownership and management, local residence, and civic participation. . . .

2

[The Court then reviewed the various actions Congress had taken in support of the minority ownership policies. Most recently, for the past three years, Congress "specifically required the Commission, through appropriations legislation, to maintain the minority ownership policies without alteration."]

C

The judgment that there is a link between expanded minority ownership and broadcast diversity does not rest on impermissible stereotyping. Congressional policy does not assume that in every case minority ownership and management will lead to more minority-oriented programming or to the expression of a discrete "minority viewpoint" on the airwaves. Neither does it pretend that all programming that appeals to minority audiences can be labeled "minority programming" or that programming that might be described as "minority" does not appeal to nonminorities. Rather, both Congress and the FCC maintain simply that expanded minority ownership of broadcast outlets will, in the aggregate, result in greater broadcast diversity. A broadcasting industry with representative minority participation will produce more variation and diversity than will one whose ownership is drawn from a single racially and ethnically homogenous group. . . .

Although all station owners are guided to some extent by market demand in their programming decisions, Congress and the Commission have determined that there may be important differences between the broadcasting practices of minority owners and those of their nonminority counterparts. This judgment--and the conclusion that there is a nexus between minority ownership and broadcasting diversity--is corroborated by a host of empirical evidence. Evidence suggests that an owner's minority status influences the selection of topics for news coverage and the presentation of editorial viewpoint, especially on matters of particular concern to minorities. "[M]inority ownership does appear to have specific impact on the presentation of minority images in local news," inasmuch as minority-owned stations tend to devote more news time to topics of minority interest and to avoid racial and ethnic stereotypes in portraying minorities. In addition, studies show that a minority owner is more likely to employ minorities in managerial and other important roles where they can have an impact on station policies. If the FCC's equal employment policies "ensure that . . .

licensees' programming fairly reflects the tastes and viewpoints of minority groups," [ ], it is difficult to deny that minority-owned stations that follow such employment policies on their own will also contribute to diversity. While we are under no illusion that members of a particular minority group share some cohesive, collective viewpoint, we believe it a legitimate inference for Congress and the Commission to draw that as more minorities gain ownership and policymaking roles in the media, varying perspectives will be more fairly represented on the airwaves. The policies are thus a product of "'analysis'" rather than a "'stereotyped reaction'" based on "'[h]abit.'"

. . .

D

We find that the minority ownership policies are in other relevant respects substantially related to the goal of promoting broadcast diversity. First, the Commission adopted and Congress endorsed minority ownership preferences only after long study and painstaking consideration of all available alternatives. [ ] . . .

. . .

Moreover, the considered nature of the Commission's judgment in selecting the particular minority ownership policies at issue today is illustrated by the fact that the Commission has rejected other types of minority preferences. For example, the Commission has studied but refused to implement the more expansive alternative of setting aside certain frequencies for minority broadcasters. [ ] In addition, in a ruling released the day after it adopted the comparative hearing credit and the distress sale preference, the FCC declined to adopt a plan to require 45-day advance public notice before a station could be sold, which had been advocated on the ground that it would ensure minorities a chance to bid on stations that might otherwise be sold to industry insiders without ever coming on the market. [ ] . . .

The minority ownership policies, furthermore, are aimed directly at the barriers that minorities face in

entering the broadcasting industry. The Commission's
Task Force identified as key factors hampering the
growth of minority ownership a lack of adequate
financing, paucity of information regarding license
availability, and broadcast inexperience. [ ] The
Commission assigned a preference to minority status in
the comparative licensing proceeding, reasoning that
such an enhancement might help to compensate for a
dearth of broadcasting experience. Most license
acquisitions, however, are by necessity purchases of
existing stations, because only a limited number of
new stations are available, and those are often in
less desirable markets or on less profitable portions
of spectrum, such as the UHF band. Congress and the
FCC therefore found a need for the minority distress
sale policy, which helps to overcome the problem of
lack of information by providing existing licensees
with an incentive to seek out minority buyers. The
Commission's choice of minority ownership policies
thus addressed the very factors it had isolated as
being responsible for minority underrepresentation in
the broadcast industry.

     . . .

    Finally, we do not believe that the minority
ownership policies at issue impose impermissible
burdens on nonminorities. Although the nonminority
challengers in these cases concede that they have not
suffered the loss of an already-awarded broadcast
license, they claim that they have been handicapped in
their ability to obtain one in the first instance.
But just as we have determined that "[a]s part of this
Nation's dedication to eradicating racial
discrimination, innocent persons may be called upon to
bear some of the burden of the remedy," [ ] we
similarly find that a congressionally mandated benign
race-conscious program that is substantially related
to the achievement of an important governmental
interest is consistent with equal protection
principles so long as it does not impose *undue* burdens
on nonminorities. [ ]

    In the context of broadcasting licenses, the
burden on nonminorities is slight. The FCC's
responsibility is to grant licenses in the "public
interest, convenience, or necessity," 47 U.S.C.
§§ 307, 309 (1982 ed.), and the limited number of

frequencies on the electromagnetic spectrum means that "[n]o one has a First Amendment right to a license." *Red Lion*, [ ]. Applicants have no settled expectation that their applications will be granted without consideration of public interest factors such as minority ownership. Award of a preference in a comparative hearing or transfer of a station in a distress sale thus contravenes "no legitimate firmly rooted expectation[s]" of competing applicants. [ ]

. . .

III

The Commission's minority ownership policies bear the imprimatur of longstanding congressional support and direction and are substantially related to the achievement of the important governmental objective of broadcast diversity. The judgment in [*Metro*] is affirmed, the judgment in [*Shurberg*] is reversed, and the cases are remanded for proceedings consistent with this opinion.

JUSTICE STEVENS, concurring.

Today the Court squarely rejects the proposition that a governmental decision that rests on a racial classification is never permissible except as a remedy for a past wrong. [ ] I endorse this focus on the future benefit, rather than the remedial justification, of such decisions.

I remain convinced, of course, that racial or ethnic characteristics provide a relevant basis for disparate treatment only in extremely rare situations and that it is therefore "especially important that the reasons for any such classification be clearly identified and unquestionably legitimate." [ ] The Court's opinion explains how both elements of that standard are satisfied. Specifically, the reason for the classification--the recognized interest in broadcast diversity--is clearly identified and does not imply any judgment concerning the abilities of owners of different races or the merits of different kinds of programming. Neither the favored nor the disfavored class is stigmatized in any way. In addition, the Court demonstrates that this case falls within the extremely narrow category of governmental decisions for which racial or ethnic heritage may provide a rational basis for differential treatment. The public interest in broadcast diversity--like the interest in an integrated police force, diversity in the composition of a public school faculty or diversity in the student body of a professional school--is in my view unquestionably legitimate.

Therefore, I join both the opinion and judgment of the Court.

JUSTICE O'CONNOR, with whom THE CHIEF JUSTICE, JUSTICE SCALIA, and JUSTICE KENNEDY join, dissenting.

At the heart of the Constitution's guarantee of equal protection lies the simple command that the Government must treat citizens "as *individuals*, not 'as simply components of a racial, religious, sexual or national class.'" [ ] Social scientists may debate how peoples' thoughts and behavior reflect their background, but the Constitution provides that the Government may not allocate benefits and burdens among individuals based on the assumption that race or ethnicity determines how they act or think. To uphold the challenged programs, the Court departs from these fundamental principles and from our traditional requirement that racial classifications are permissible only if necessary and narrowly tailored to achieve a compelling interest. This departure marks a renewed toleration of racial classifications and a repudiation of our recent affirmation that the Constitution's equal protection guarantees extend equally to all citizens. The Court's application of a lessened equal protection standard to congressional action finds no support in our cases or in the Constitution. I respectfully dissent.

I

As we recognized last Term, the Constitution requires that the Court apply a strict standard of scrutiny to evaluate racial classifications such as those contained in the challenged FCC distress sale and comparative licensing policies. [ ] . . .

. . .

Nor does the congressional role in prolonging the FCC's policies justify any lower level of scrutiny. As with all instances of judicial review of federal legislation, the Court does not lightly set aside the considered judgment of a coordinate branch. Nonetheless, the respect due a coordinate branch yields neither less vigilance in defense of equal protection principles nor any corresponding diminution of the standard of review. . . .

. . .

II

Our history reveals the most blatant forms of discrimination have been visited upon some members of the racial and ethnic groups identified in the challenged programs. Many have lacked the opportunity to share in the Nation's wealth and to participate in its commercial enterprises. It is undisputed that minority participation in the broadcasting industry falls markedly below the demographic representation of those groups, [ ], and this shortfall may be traced in part to the discrimination and the patterns of exclusion that have widely affected our society. . . .

. . .

III

Under the appropriate standard, strict scrutiny, only a compelling interest may support the Government's use of racial classifications. Modern equal protection doctrine has recognized only one such interest: remedying the effects of racial discrimination. The interest in increasing the diversity of broadcast viewpoints is clearly not a compelling interest. It is simply too amorphous, too insubstantial, and too unrelated to any legitimate basis for employing racial classifications. The Court does not claim otherwise. Rather, it employs its novel standard and claims that this asserted interest need only be, and is, "important." . . .

An interest capable of justifying race-conscious measures must be sufficiently specific and verifiable, such that it supports only limited and carefully defined uses of racial classifications. . . .

. . . The [asserted] interest [in this case] is certainly amorphous: the FCC and the majority of this Court understandably do not suggest how one would define or measure a particular viewpoint that might be associated with race, or even how one would assess the diversity of broadcast viewpoints. . . . [T]he interest would support indefinite use of racial classifications, employed first to obtain the appropriate mixture of racial views and then to ensure that the broadcasting spectrum continues to reflect that mixture. We cannot deem to be constitutionally adequate an interest that would support measures that amount to the core constitutional violation of "outright racial balancing." [ ]

The asserted interest would justify discrimination against members of any group found to contribute to an insufficiently diverse broadcasting spectrum, including those groups currently favored. [We have previously] rejected as insufficiently weighty the interest in achieving role models in public schools, in part because that rationale could as readily be used to limit the hiring of teachers who belonged to particular minority groups. [ ] The FCC's claimed interest could similarly justify limitations on minority members' participation in broadcasting. It would be unwise to depend upon the Court's restriction of its holding to "benign" measures to forestall this result. Divorced from any remedial purpose and otherwise undefined, "benign" means only what shifting fashions and changing politics deem acceptable. Members of any racial or ethnic group, whether now preferred under the FCC's policies or not, may find themselves politically out of fashion and subject to disadvantageous but "benign" discrimination.

Under the majority's holding, the FCC may also advance its asserted interest in viewpoint diversity by identifying what constitutes a "Black viewpoint," an "Asian viewpoint," an "Arab viewpoint," and so on; determining which viewpoints are underrepresented; and then using that determination to mandate particular programming or to deny licenses to those deemed by virtue of their race or ethnicity less likely to present the favored views.   Indeed, the FCC has, if taken at its word, essentially pursued this course, albeit without making express its reasons for choosing to favor particular groups or for concluding that the broadcasting spectrum is insufficiently diverse.   [ ]

　　　. . .

Even considered as other than a justification for using race classifications, the asserted interest in viewpoint diversity falls short of being weighty enough.   The Court has recognized an interest in obtaining diverse broadcasting viewpoints as a legitimate basis for the FCC, acting pursuant to its "public interest" statutory mandate, to adopt limited measures to increase the number of competing licensees and to encourage licensees to present varied views on issues of public concern.   See, e.g., [NCCB]; [Red Lion]; [Storer Broadcasting]; [AP]; [NBC].   We have also concluded that these measures do not run afoul of the First Amendment's usual prohibition of Government regulation of the marketplace of ideas, in part because First Amendment concerns support limited but inevitable Government regulation of the peculiarly constrained broadcasting spectrum.   [Red Lion]   But the conclusion that measures adopted to further the interest in diversity of broadcasting viewpoints are neither beyond the FCC's statutory authority nor contrary to the First Amendment hardly establishes the interest as important for equal protection purposes.

The FCC's extension of the asserted interest in diversity of views in this case presents, at the very least, an unsettled First Amendment issue.   The FCC has concluded that the American broadcasting public receives the incorrect mix of ideas and claims to have adopted the challenged policies to supplement programming content with a particular set of views. Although we have approved limited measures designed to increase information and views generally, the Court has never upheld a broadcasting measure designed to amplify a distinct set of views or the views of a particular class of speakers.   Indeed, the Court has suggested that the First Amendment prohibits allocating licenses to further such ends.   See [NBC] ("But Congress did not authorize the Commission to choose among [license] applicants on the basis of their political, economic or social views, or upon any

other capricious basis. If it did, or if the
Commission by these Regulations proposed a choice
among applicants upon some such basis, the [First
Amendment] issue before us would be totally
different"). Even if an interest is determined to be
legitimate in one context, it does not suddenly become
important enough to justify distinctions based on
race.

IV

Our traditional equal protection doctrine
requires, in addition to a compelling state interest,
that the Government's chosen means be necessary to
accomplish and narrowly tailored to further the
asserted interest. [ ] . . .

1

The FCC claims to advance its asserted interest
in diverse viewpoints by singling out race and
ethnicity as peculiarly linked to distinct views that
require enhancement. The FCC's choice to employ a
racial criterion embodies the related notions that a
particular and distinct viewpoint inheres in certain
racial groups, and that a particular applicant, by
virtue of race or ethnicity alone, is more valued than
other applicants because "likely to provide [that]
distinct perspective." [ ] The policies directly
equate race with belief and behavior, for they
establish race as a necessary and sufficient condition
of securing the preference. . . .

The FCC assumes a particularly strong correlation
of race and behavior. The FCC justifies its
conclusion that insufficiently diverse viewpoints are
broadcast by reference to the percentage of minority
owned stations. This assumption is correct only to
the extent that minority owned stations provide the
desired additional views, and that stations owned by
individuals not favored by the preferences cannot, or
at least do not, broadcast underrepresented
programming. Additionally, the FCC's focus on
ownership to improve programming assumes that
preferences linked to race are so strong that they
will dictate the owner's behavior in operating the
station, overcoming the owner's personal inclinations
and regard for the market. . . .

. . .   The Court embraces the FCC's reasoning
that an applicant's race will likely indicate that the
applicant possesses a distinct perspective, but notes
that the correlation of race to behavior is "not a
rigid assumption about how minority owners will behave
in every case." [ ] The corollary to this notion is
plain: individuals of unfavored racial and ethnic
backgrounds are unlikely to possess the unique
experiences and background that contribute to
viewpoint diversity. Both the reasoning and its
corollary reveal but disregard what is objectionable
about a stereotype: the racial generalization
inevitably does not apply to certain individuals, and
those persons may legitimately claim that they have
been judged according to their race rather than upon
a relevant criterion. [ ] Similarly disturbing is
the majority's reasoning that different treatment on
the basis of race is permissible because efficacious
"in the aggregate." [ ] . . . This reliance on the
"aggregate" and on probabilities confirms that the
Court has abandoned heightened scrutiny, which
requires a direct rather than approximate fit of means
to ends. We would not tolerate the Government's claim
that hiring persons of a particular race leads to
better service "in the aggregate," and we should not
accept as legitimate the FCC's claim in this case that
members of certain races will provide superior
programming, even if "in the aggregate." The
Constitution's text, our cases, and our Nation's
history foreclose such premises.

2

Moreover, the FCC's selective focus on viewpoints
associated with race illustrates a particular
tailoring difficulty. The asserted interest is in
advancing the Nation's different "social, political,
esthetic, moral, and other ideas and experiences," *Red
Lion*, [ ], yet of all the varied traditions and ideas
shared among our citizens, the FCC has sought to
amplify only those particular views it identifies
through the classifications most suspect under equal
protection doctrine. Even if distinct views could be
associated with particular ethnic and racial groups,
focusing on this particular aspect of the Nation's
views calls into question the Government's genuine
commitment to its asserted interest. [ ]

. . . The policy is overinclusive: many members of a particular racial or ethnic group will have no interest in advancing the views the FCC believes to be underrepresented, or will find them utterly foreign. The policy is underinclusive: it awards no preference to disfavored individuals who may be particularly well versed in and committed to presenting those views. The FCC has failed to implement a case-by-case determination, and that failure is particularly unjustified when individualized hearings already occur, as in the comparative licensing process. [ ] . . .

Moreover, the FCC's programs cannot survive even intermediate scrutiny because race-neutral and untried means of directly accomplishing the governmental interest are readily available. The FCC could directly advance its interest by requiring licensees to provide programming that the FCC believes would add to diversity. The interest the FCC asserts is in programming diversity, yet in adopting the challenged policies, the FCC expressly disclaimed having attempted *any* direct efforts to achieve its asserted goal. [ ] . . . The FCC and the Court suggest that First Amendment interests in some manner should exempt the FCC from employing this direct, race-neutral means to achieve its asserted interest. They essentially argue that we may bend our equal protection principles to avoid more readily apparent harm to our First Amendment values. But the FCC cannot have it both ways: either the First Amendment bars the FCC from seeking to accomplish indirectly what it may not accomplish directly; or the FCC may pursue the goal, but must do so in a manner that comports with equal protection principles. And if the FCC can direct programming in any fashion, it must employ that direct means before resorting to indirect race-conscious means.

Other race-neutral means also exist, and all are at least as direct as the FCC's racial classifications. The FCC could evaluate applicants upon their ability to provide and commitment to offer whatever programming the FCC believes would reflect underrepresented viewpoints. If the FCC truly seeks diverse programming rather than allocation of goods to persons of particular racial backgrounds, it has little excuse to look to racial background rather than programming to further the programming interest. Additionally, if the FCC believes that certain persons by virtue of their unique experiences will contribute as owners to more diverse broadcasting, the FCC could simply favor applicants whose particular background indicates that they, will add to the diversity of programming, rather than rely solely upon suspect classifications. Also, race-neutral means exist to allow access to the broadcasting industry for those persons excluded for financial and related reasons. The Court reasons that various minority preferences, including those reflected in the distress sale, overcome barriers of information, experience, and financing that inhibit minority ownership. [ ] Race-neutral financial and informational measures most directly reduce financial and informational barriers.

. . .

The FCC has posited a relative absence of "minority viewpoints," yet it has never suggested what those views might be, or what other viewpoints might be absent from the broadcasting spectrum. It has never identified any particular deficiency in programming diversity that should be the subject of greater programming, or that necessitates racial classifications.

. . .

The FCC seeks to avoid the tailoring difficulties by focusing on minority ownership rather than the asserted interest in diversity of broadcast viewpoints. The Constitution clearly prohibits allocating valuable goods such as broadcast licenses simply on the basis of race. [ ] Yet the FCC refers to the lack of minority ownership to support the existence of a lack of diversity of viewpoints, and has fitted its programs to increase ownership. [ ] This repeated focus on ownership supports the inference that the FCC seeks to allocate licenses based on race, an impermissible end, rather than to increase diversity of viewpoints, the asserted interest. And this justification that links the use of race preferences to minority ownership rather than to diversity of viewpoints ensure's that the FCC's programs . . . "cannot be tailored to any goal, except perhaps outright racial balancing."

3

. . .

Three difficulties suggest that the nexus between owners' race and programming is considerably less than substantial. First, the market shapes programming to a tremendous extent. Members of minority groups who own licenses might be thought, like other owners, to seek to broadcast programs that will attract and retain audiences, rather than programs that reflect the owner's tastes and preferences. [ ] Second, station owners have only limited control over the content of programming. The distress sale presents a particularly acute difficulty of this sort. Unlike the comparative licensing program, the distress sale policy provides preferences to minority owners who neither intend nor desire to manage the station in any respect. [ ] Whatever distinct programming may attend the race of an owner actively involved in managing the station, an absentee owner would have far less effect on programming.

Third, the FCC had absolutely no factual basis for the nexus when it adopted the policies and has since established none to support its existence.
. . .

. . .

4

Finally, the Government cannot employ race classifications that unduly burden individuals who are not members of the favored racial and ethnic groups. [ ] The challenged policies fail this independent requirement, as well as the other constitutional requirements. The comparative licensing and distress sale programs provide the eventual licensee with an exceptionally valuable property and with a rare and unique opportunity to serve the local community. The distress sale imposes a particularly significant burden. The FCC has at base created a specialized market reserved exclusively for minority controlled applicants. There is no more rigid quota than a 100% set-aside. . . . The Court's argument that the distress sale allocates only a small percentage of all license sales, [ ], also misses the mark. This argument readily supports complete preferences and avoids scrutiny of particular programs: it is no response to a person denied admission at one school, or discharged from one job, solely on the basis of race, that other schools or employers do not discriminate.

The comparative licensing program, too, imposes a significant burden. The Court's emphasis on the multifactor process should not be confused with the claim that the preference is in some sense a minor one. It is not. The basic nonrace criteria are not difficult to meet, and, given the sums at stake, applicants have every incentive to structure their ownership arrangement to prevail in the comparative process. Applicants cannot alter their race, of course, and race is clearly the dispositive factor in a substantial percentage of comparative proceedings. Petitioner Metro asserts that race is overwhelmingly the dispositive factor. In reply, the FCC admits that it has not assessed the operation of its own program, [ ], and the Court notes only that "minority ownership does not guarantee that an applicant will prevail." [ ]

. . . I respectfully dissent.

JUSTICE KENNEDY, with whom JUSTICE SCALIA joins, dissenting.

[Justice Kennedy compared this case with Plessy v. Ferguson, in which the Court found constitutional a Louisiana law requiring "equal but separate accommodations" for railroad passengers of different races.]

. . . All that need be shown under the new approach . . . is that the future effect of discriminating among citizens on the basis of race will advance some "important" governmental interest.

Once the Government takes the step, which itself should be forbidden, of enacting into law the stereotypical assumption that the race of the owners is linked to broadcast content, it must decide which races to favor. While the Court repeatedly refers to the preferences as favoring "minorities," [ ], and purports to evaluate the burdens imposed on "nonminorities," [ ], it must be emphasized that the discriminatory policies upheld today to exclude the many racial and ethnic *minorities* that have not made the Commission's list. The enumeration of the races to be protected is borrowed from a remedial statute, but since the remedial rationale must be disavowed in order to sustain the policy, the race classifications bear scant relation to the asserted governmental interest. The Court's reasoning provides little justification for welcoming the return of racial classifications to our Nation's laws.

. . .

. . . Perhaps the Court can succeed in its assumed role of case-by-case arbiter of when it is desirable and benign for the Government to disfavor some citizens and favor others based on the color of their skin. Perhaps the tolerance and decency to which our people aspire will let the disfavored rise above hostility and the favored escape condescension. But history suggests much peril in this enterprise, and so the Constitution forbids us to undertake it. I regret that after a century of judicial opinions we interpret the Constitution to do no more than move us from "separate but equal" to "unequal but benign."

Notes and Questions

1. What effect does *Metro Broadcasting* have on the ongoing debate over the continuing viability of the scarcity rationale?

2. *Metro Broadcasting* did not settle the question of whether the female preference policy is constitutional. That issue was argued before the Court of Appeals for the District of Columbia Circuit in Lambrecht v. Federal Communications Commission. The case is attracting increased attention because Supreme Court nominee Clarence Thomas is a member of the panel deciding the case. Broadcasting, July 8, 1991 at 26.

Add to casebook p. 187, after 2nd full paragraph:

The consent decrees expired on Nov. 14, 1990. United States v. National Broadcasting Co., 449 F.Supp. 1127

(D.C.Ca.1978); United States v. Columbia Broadcasting
System, Inc., 45 Fed.Reg. 34,463 (1980); United States
v. American Broadcasting Cos., 45 Fed.Reg. 58,441
(1980).

Add to casebook p. 202, after note 6:

6a. Since adoption of the original financial interest
and syndication rules and PTAR the FCC has granted two
permanent waivers.   The first allows the Christian
Broadcast Network (CBN) to provide up to 30 hours of
weekly programming without being subject to those
rules.   Christian Broadcasting Network, Inc., 87
F.C.C.2d 1076, 50 R.R.2d 359 (1981).   The second
exempts the Home Shopping Network (HSN) from the dual
network rule and PTAR.   Home Shopping, Inc., 4
F.C.C.Rcd. 2422, 66 R.R.2d 175 (1989).   According to
the Commission the waivers were justified by the fact
that neither CBN nor HSN was significantly involved in
either the sale of national advertising or the
production, acquisition or distribution of traditional
entertainment programs to commercial stations for
airing during the prime-time-access period.

6b.   The attempt by Fox Television to establish a
fourth network, p. 55 (the casebook), *supra*, forced
the Commission to return to the issue of the financial
interest and syndication rules.   The rules did not
initially apply to Fox because its early programming
was not sufficient to meet the existing FCC definition
of a network, 47 C.F.R. § 73.658(j)(4), p. 204 (the
casebook), *infra*.   Although Fox was providing
programming to more than 25 affiliates in more than 10
states, it was providing only nine hours a week of
such programming.   However, after announcing plans to
increase its programming efforts to 18 1/2 hours a
week by the fall 1990 television season, Fox filed a
petition asking the FCC to resume rulemaking in the
financial interest and syndication rules proceeding.

       In response the Commission terminated the old
rulemaking proceeding as "stale" and issued a new NPRM
on the financial interest and syndication rules.   In
the NPRM the Commission sought comment on five
different options. The first was to make no change in
either rule.   The second was to eliminate the
financial interest rule while leaving the syndication

rule unchanged. The third suggested alternative was
to eliminate the financial interest rule and amend the
syndication rule to apply only to domestic syndication
of prime-time series. A fourth possibility suggested
was elimination of the financial interest rule while
amending the syndication rule to permit network
syndication of a certain number or percentage of
programs or to share in profits of non-network
syndicators. The final option on which comments were
sought was to leave the rules themselves unchanged,
but to provide an exception for "emerging networks."
Evaluation of the Syndication and Financial Interest
Rules, 5 F.C.C.Rcd. 1815 (1990).

6c.   The NPRM on the financial interest and
syndication rules elicited thousands upon thousands of
pages of comments.   These comments presented
"alternative views of the television programming world
so starkly and fundamentally at odds with each other
that they virtually defy reconciliation."   The
Commission itself was sharply divided on the issue.
Although the commissioners all agreed that the video
marketplace had changed dramatically in the 20 years
since the original rules were adopted, they did not
agree on the degree to which that change rendered
those rules unnecessary.   By a 3-2 vote, the
Commission decided to retain the rules, but with
substantial modifications which it summarized as
follows:

> 17. In particular, by this *Report and Order*, we
> take the following actions to enhance the
> ability of existing and emerging networks to
> compete effectively in today's video
> marketplace, but not dominate it unfairly.
>
> --   The financial interest and syndication
>   rules will no longer be applied to non-
>   entertainment programming (*e.g.*, news and
>   sports) in prime time, nor to any network
>   programming outside of prime time. These
>   rules, as modified, will continue to govern
>   production, acquisition and syndication of
>   network prime time entertainment programs
>   and network participation in first-run
>   syndication.

-- A network may acquire financial interests, domestic syndication rights and foreign syndication rights in any outside productions aired on its prime time entertainment schedule, provided that (1) such rights are purchased pursuant to separate negotiations initiated no less than 30 days after execution of the network license fee agreement (and, where applicable, a pilot production agreement); and (2) the network certifies that access to its schedule was not conditioned on the acquisition of such rights.

-- A network may produce up to 40 percent of its prime time entertainment schedule "in house" (*i.e.*, "solely produced" or co-produced" by the network, as defined herein), and it may retain financial interests and active syndication rights, both domestic and foreign, in those productions. Co-production arrangements between the network and a domestic producer may be initiated only by the outside producer, who shall be provided a 30-day cooling-off period before the arrangement becomes binding.

-- Networks may not favor their affiliates nor unduly delay the syndication of those "in-house" productions they actively distribute in the domestic marketplace.

-- A network may produce in-house an unlimited amount of prime time entertainment programming for airing or distribution on other broadcast networks or other broadcast outlets, and it may retain financial interests and foreign and domestic syndication rights in such programs. However, these programs may be syndicated domestically only through an independent syndicator subject to safeguards.

-- Networks shall be allowed to engage in foreign distribution of programming free of any distribution safeguards.

--   A network may produce first-run programming
       and retain financial interests and foreign
       syndication rights in such programming
       "solely produced" in-house, but may
       domestically distribute such programming
       only through an independent syndicator
       subject to safeguards. A network may not
       acquire any financial interests or
       syndication rights from outside producers
       of domestic first-run syndication
       programming.

--   For purposes of these rules, a network will
       be defined as any entity providing more
       than 15 hours per week of prime time
       programming on a regular basis to
       interconnected affiliates that reach, in
       aggregate, at least 75 percent of
       television households nationwide.

--   A new network's program ownership rights
       obtained prior to becoming a "network"
       shall be "grandfathered." A new network
       and its affiliates will have a transition
       period of 36 months to bring pre-existing
       contracts into compliance with the prime
       time access rule. A new network otherwise
       shall be required to comply immediately
       with the new rules.

--   A network must maintain semi-annual reports
       in its owned and operated stations' public
       files. These reports must include network
       certification of its compliance with the
       instant rules and other specific
       information regarding prime time
       entertainment programs which it has
       produced or aired or in which it holds
       financial interests or syndication rights.

--   These rules shall be reviewed by the
       Commission four years from their effective
       date.

       The decision to limit the rules to prime-time
programming and first-run syndication was based on the
conclusion that this is only programming for which a
strong syndication markets exist. Prime-time

programming is defined as programming that "has network exhibition during the hours of 7 p.m. to 11 p.m. eastern time and pacific time, or 6 p.m. to 10 p.m. central time and mountain time.

With regard to the financial interest rule, the Commission concluded that although the networks no longer have the almost total dominance of 20 years ago, they still have sufficient power to extract rights from program producers in return for network exhibition. At the same time, the FCC determined that the existing financial interest rule was disserving "the public interest in diversity by limiting the funding of new, outside programming." The solution was to allow networks to obtain financial interests in prime-time entertainment programming subject to the "antiextraction" safeguards--separate negotiations 30 days apart and certification--noted above.

The 40 percent cap on in-house production also represents a balance between the recognition of the reduced power of the networks and a fear that sufficient power remains for the networks engage in anticompetitive practices. More specifically, the cap was justified as serving three public interest goals. First, it will "curb potential network syndication abuses while at the same time assessing the actual impact of limited network involvement in that marketplace. Second, it would limit the ability of the networks "to coerce outside producers to produce programs in-house." Finally, allowing networks to produce their entire prime-time schedule in-house would reduce diversity of viewpoints.

The extraction concerns that led to the financial interest safeguards also convinced the Commission to apply the same safeguards to domestic syndication. In addition, to prevent networks from "warehousing" (unduly withholding them from the syndication market) their product, the FCC imposed a requirement that networks must release programs into the syndication market "after four years or within six months following the end of the network run, whichever is sooner. However, the Commission did not have the same concerns regarding foreign syndication and thus, eliminated all restrictions on network participation in foreign syndication.

The two dissenters, Sykes and Quello, both felt that the Commission did not go nearly far enough in relaxing the rules. In separate dissents, each argued that the networks no longer have sufficient market power to exercise any significant control over the prime-time programming market. Thus, in their opinion, the Commission should have substantially, if not totally repealed the rules. In support of his argument that the networks no longer have sufficient market power, Sykes cited the following comparative statistics:

> The video marketplace of 1991 bears not even a superficial resemblance to the marketplace that existed in 1970 when the rules were originally adopted. Even today's majority concedes this point. The number of television stations has grown by more than 500 since 1970, and television advertising revenues have increased from $3.6 billion to $26.9 billion. In 1970 there were only 65 independent stations; now there are 339. This expansion in the number of independent stations has provided a nucleus for a fourth television network, The Fox Network. Cable television, a negligible presence in 1970, has since become the means whereby the majority of American households view television. Cable now serves 59 percent of the national television audience, and is available to about 90 percent of it. As a result, the average American viewer can now access 30 channels of television, as opposed to 7 in 1970. Not surprisingly, yearly cable subscriber revenues have grown from $300 million in 1970 to $16.2 billion today, and cable advertising revenues total $2.5 billion per year. It is estimated that cable revenues from local advertising and pay-per-view services will grow from 15 to 50 percent *each year*. The number of national cable program services has grown from zero in 1970 to 90 today. Today there are 3 million home satellite dish users and over 70 percent of American homes have VCRs; neither dishes nor VCRs were in use in 1970.

Financial Interest and Syndication Rules, 69 R.R.2d 341 (1991).

CBS and NBC filed petitions for reconsideration seeking much greater relaxation of the rules. Meanwhile, the Coalition to Preserve the Financial Interest and Syndication Rule, joined by various representatives of program producers and independent television stations, files petitions for reconsideration claiming the rules had been relaxed too much, especially with regard to the antiextraction safeguards and limitations on in-house made-for-TV movies and mini-series. ABC did not join the other networks in their petition, choosing instead to file an appeal in the District of Columbia circuit. Broadcasting, July 15, 1991 at 29. Previously, the Media Access Project had filed an appeal in the ninth circuit; the CBS Television Network Affiliates Association and Fox Broadcasting had filed appeals in the District of Columbia circuit; and Schurz Communications Inc., licensee of a CBS affiliate, had filed an appeal in the seventh circuit. Broadcasting, June 24, 1991 at 55.

Chapter VI

LEGAL CONTROL OF BROADCAST PROGRAMMING:
POLITICAL SPEECH

Add to casebook p. 223, after 4th full paragraph:

In July 1990 the Mass Media Bureau conducted an audit of 30 television and radio stations to determine the level of compliance with the political programming rules, particularly the lowest unit rate requirement. In September 1990 it issued a preliminary report on the results of its audit. The Bureau found that, "at sixteen of the twenty audited television stations (80%), candidates paid more for broadcast time than commercial advertisers in virtually every daypart or program time period analyzed. Indeed, candidates sometimes paid more than every commercial advertiser aired in the same dayparts. Candidates fared better on radio, paying more than commercial advertisers at only four of the eight audited stations that sold time to candidates."

The primary cause of the disparity was the fact that candidates tended to buy non-preemptible, fixed-time commercials. This assured that the candidates' commercials would not only run, but would do so at the exact times they wanted. In contrast, commercial advertisers tended to buy preemptible commercials. Because they were willing to risk that their commercials might be preempted if enough non-preemptible commercials were sold, they paid a lower rate. Technically, preemptible commercials are a different class of time, and thus, selling them at a lower rate is not a violation of the lowest unit rate requirement. However, the Bureau indicated a concern that candidates were not being given adequate information regarding the likelihood that a preemptible commercial would in fact be preempted and the availability of "make good" commercials in the event that preemptions did occur.

Based on its preliminary findings the Bureau urged broadcasters to "disclose to candidates all rates and the availability of package options available to commercial advertisers. . . . This disclosure should specify all discount privileges, including every level of preemptibility, the approximate clearance potential of time purchased at current effective selling levels, and special package plans.   The disclosure should also indicate the station's policies with respect to make goods and the availability of negotiating for time if that is the practice with commercial advertisers."   Political Programming Audit, 68 R.R.2d 113 (M.M.Bur.1990).

The audit resulted in further questions from both candidates and broadcasters still seemingly confused over the exact requirements of the lowest unit rate provision of the Act.   In mid-1991 the FCC issued an NPRM aimed at clearing up the confusion.   Among the questions addressed in the NPRM are what constitutes a distinct class of time, how to "calculate the lowest unit charge when using a variety of different option privileges and discounts," and how much disclosure of the various option privileges and discounts should be made to political candidates.

The audit also proposes a stricter sponsorship identification requirement as a prerequisite for candidates availing themselves of the lowest unit rate.   Under the proposal, sponsoring candidates' pictures would have to fill a minimum of 20 percent of the screen for at least six seconds.   Broadcasting, June 17, 1991 at 21.

An additional impetus for the Commission's action was a group of law suits filed by political candidates against various Alabama and Georgia television stations alleging overcharges in violation of the lowest-unit-rate requirement.   The cases have been complicated by conflicting rulings by federal district courts in the two states on the question of whether the FCC has exclusive jurisdiction over lowest-unit-rate violations.   The candidates have also filed complaints with the FCC.   Broadcasting, July 8, 1991 at 52.

Add to casebook p. 229, after note 2:

3. After *CBS*, the general rule for federal candidates is that broadcasters cannot establish across-the-board policies, but rather must consider the particular

needs of each individual candidate. There is one exception to that, however. Stations may establish a policy of not selling any political advertisements during news programming. Commission Policy in Enforcing Section 312(a)(7), 68 F.C.C.2d 1079, 43 R.R.2d 1079 (1978). In its 1991 political access NPRM, p. 45 (this supplement), *supra*, the FCC has asked whether it should continue that exception.

Add Syracuse Peace Council v. Federal Communications Commission which is in Appendix D (the casebook), to page 266, after 1st paragraph.

Add to casebook p. 266, replacing note 1:

1. Under the majority's view, how might a new fairness doctrine come into being? Under Judge Starr's view, what would it take to bring a new fairness doctrine into being?

1a. On the constitutional side, what does Judge Starr's discussion of "scarcity" add to the discussion in *Red Lion*?

Add to casebook p. 269, replacing note 3:

3. If bill similar to S. 742 should be enacted, how should a court treat its findings in a case challenging its constitutionality? Do the Congressional "findings" make the FCC's "findings" irrelevant?

Chapter VII

LEGAL CONTROL OF BROADCAST PROGRAMMING:
NONPOLITICAL SPEECH

Add to casebook p. 315, after note 3:

3a. Both proponents and opponents of the 24-hour-a-day ban had hoped that the Supreme Court might provide support for their position in a case involving "dial-a-porn," prerecorded pornographic messages available to telephone callers for a small per-call fee. In 1988 Congress had attempted to abolish dial-a-porn by making it a crime to provide obscene or indecent commercial telephone messages in interstate commerce. The Supreme Court unanimously held the statute unconstitutional insofar as it proscribed material that was not obscene:

>   Sexual expression which is indecent but not obscene is protected by the First Amendment, and the government does not submit that the sale of such materials to adults could be criminalized solely because they are indecent. The government may, however, regulate the content of constitutionally protected speech in order to promote a compelling interest if it chooses the least restrictive means to further the articulated interest. We have recognized that there is a compelling interest in protecting the physical well-being of minors. This interest extends to shielding minors from the influence of literature that is not obscene by adult standards. [ ] The government may serve this legitimate interest, but to withstand constitutional scrutiny, "it must do so by narrowly drawn regulations designed to serve those interests without unnecessarily interfering with First Amendment freedoms." [ ]

The government argued that a total ban on dial-a-porn was the only effective way to prevent it from reaching minors, because enterprising youngsters would find some way to avoid lesser restrictions such as codes, scrambling procedures, or access by credit card only. The Court refused to defer to Congress's view on that point, noting that both the FCC and the court of appeals had concluded that the lesser restrictions would be "feasible and effective" in preventing access by children. Sable Communications, Inc. v. Federal Communications Commission, 109 S.Ct. 2829, 16 Med.L.Rptr. 1961 (1989).

The Court in *Sable* did not make any specific reference to the pending dispute over broadcast indecency. In August 1989, 17 media groups, relying heavily on *Sable* and the earlier decision of the court of appeals, filed briefs challenging the constitutionality of the 24-hour ban on indecent broadcast speech.

The Commission then asked the court of appeals to remand the case involving the 24-hour ban to the Commission to give it a chance to build a record justifying the ban. In September 1989, over the opposition of the media challengers, the court of appeals remanded the case to the Commission for a "full and fair" inquiry on the ban.

In late 1989 the Commission issued an NOI soliciting public comment on the validity of a total ban on broadcast indecency. The FCC asserted two government interests served by indecency regulation: "protecting children from exposure to indecent material" and "assisting parents in supervising their children." The Commission asked for comments as to whether the 24-hour ban would advance these interests.

> 17. The more difficult issue is whether a record can be developed to demonstrate that a 24-hour ban is a sufficiently limited means of restricting children's access to indecent broadcasts. In order to develop such a record, we need to compile information on many interrelated subjects, such as: (1) children's access to the broadcast media as well as their actual viewing and listening habits; (2) the feasibility of alternative means of restricting children's access to broadcasts, including time channeling alone or in conjunction with parental supervision, ratings or warning devices or alternative broadcast technologies; and (3) the availability of indecent material for adults through non-broadcast means.

Noting the court's criticism in *ACT I* of the reliance on data regarding children ages 12 to 17 even though the Commission's 1976 legislative proposal defined children as 12 or younger, the Commission started the NOI by adopting a definition of children as ages 17 and younger. The Commission then asked for information on both children's access to the broadcast media as well as their actual listening and viewing habits. Included in this was information regarding VCR use, specifically: "(1) the availability of VCR equipment to children; (2) the ability of children to use VCR equipment; and (3) children's actual use of the equipment for delayed viewing."

The Commission then asked for comments on alternatives to a 24-hour ban, "including: (1) channeling indecent broadcasts to a time of day when children most likely will not be exposed to them, including reliance on parental supervision to protect children; (2) program rating codes or pre-broadcast warning devices; and (3) feasible technologies that can be used to keep indecent broadcasts from children."

The only specific technology suggested was the Second Audio Program (SAP) channel which allows TVs equipped with a decoder to receive a different audio track for a program, The Commission asked whether putting the indecent audio on the SAP channel would sufficiently restrict access to children or would the decoders become so common as to make the SAP broadcast as accessible as regular broadcast signals. The FCC also asked whether a locking device for the SAP channel would be feasible.

Finally, the Commission asked for comments on whether a 24-hour ban would impermissibly infringe on adult's First Amendment rights:

> . . . [W]e seek comment on whether non-broadcast alternatives, including cable with a lock-box capacity, videocassettes, audiocassettes, records, motion pictures, theatres and nightclubs, provide adults with sufficient access to visual and audio indecency. Do the costs associated with each alternative reduce its practical availability to adults? Are there

differences in the types of alternatives available for video versus audio indecency?

Enforcement of Prohibitions Against Broadcast Indecency in 18 U.S.C. § 1464, R.R. Current Service 53:475 (1989).

In July 1990, the Commission unanimously adopted a report supporting a 24-hour-a-day ban on indecency for both radio and television. The report was filed with the court of appeals which will now decide whether such a ban is constitutional. In its report the Commission argued that because children are part of the broadcast audience 24 hours a day, time channeling would be ineffective in promoting the government's interest in protecting children from indecent programming. The Commission also rejected the use of technological restrictions such as limiting indecency to the SAP channel.

Given the ineffectiveness of less restrictive means of protecting children, the Commission concluded that the 24-hour ban would be a narrowly tailored way of serving a compelling government. Thus, according to the Commission, the ban was constitutional under the test adopted by the Supreme Court in *Sable*, p. 47 (this supplement), *supra*.

In a concurrence, Commissioner Quello expressed concern over the lack of empirical evidence regarding the viewing habits of children 12 years old and under. Given the fact the courts have never upheld a total ban on indecency in any medium, Quello felt that the additional evidence was needed. Broadcasting, July 16, 1990 at 30. The Commission's action was appealed.

ACTION FOR CHILDREN'S TELEVISION v. FEDERAL COMMUNICATIONS COMMISSION
United States Court of Appeals, District of Columbia Circuit, 1991.
___ F.2d ___, 69 R.R.2d 179, 18 Med.L.Rptr. 2152.

Before MIKVA, CHIEF JUDGE, EDWARDS and THOMAS, CIRCUIT JUDGES.

MIKVA, CHIEF JUDGE:

This case presents constitutional challenges to a Federal Communications Commission ("FCC" or "the Commission") order, promulgated at the direction of

Congress, barring all radio and television broadcasts of "indecent" material. We believe that the disposition of this case is governed by our prior decision in [*Action for Children's Television* (ACT I), p. 309 (the casebook), *supra*], in which we rejected vagueness and overbreadth challenges to the Commission's definition of indecency but found that the Commission's curtailment of "safe harbor" broadcast periods impermissibly intruded on constitutionally protected expression interests. Accordingly, we grant the petition for review.

I.

The particulars of this case are best understood within the history of government efforts to regulate the broadcast of indecent material. [The court then summarized the history of indecency regulation, up to and including *Pacifica*, p. 287 (the casebook).]

By 1987, however, the Commission had concluded that "the highly restrictive enforcement standard employed after the 1975 *Pacifica* decision was unduly narrow as a matter of law and inconsistent with our enforcement responsibilities under Section 1464." [In re Infinity Broadcasting Corp. of Pennsylvania, 3 F.C.C.Rcd. 930 (1987).] Returning to the generic definition of indecency it had developed in *Pacifica*, the Commission issued three rulings declaring material that would not have violated the "Filthy Words" test to be indecent. [ ] Significantly, two of the cited broadcasts had aired after 10:00 p.m., the time period previously identified by the Commission as a "safe harbor" during which the risk of children in the broadcast audience was thought to be minimal. [ ] On reconsideration, the Commission affirmed its warnings with respect to the three broadcasts and noted, in response to requests for more specific rules regarding time channeling, that 12:00 midnight was its "current thinking" as to when the risk of children in the broadcast audience could reasonably be thought minimized. [ ]

Reviewing the Commission's order, we first rejected petitioners' vagueness and overbreadth challenges to the Commission's generic definition of indecency. *ACT I* However, we vacated the Commission's rulings that the two post-10:00 p.m.

broadcasts were indecent. In addition to calling the Commission's findings "more ritual than real" and its underlying evidence "insubstantial," *id.* at 1341-42, we opined that a "reasonably safe harbor rule" was constitutionally mandated. *Id.* at 1343 n.18. Accordingly, we instructed the Commission to determine on remand, "after a full and fair hearing, . . . the times at which indecent material may be broadcast." *Id.* at 1344.

Before the Commission could carry out this court's mandate, Congress intervened. On October 1, 1988, two months after the *ACT I* decision issued, the President signed into law a 1989 appropriations bill containing the following rider:

> By January 31, 1989, the Federal Communications Commission shall promulgate regulations in accordance with section 1464, title 18, United States Code, to *enforce the provisions of such section on a 24 hour per day basis.*

Pub. L. No. 100-459, §608, 102 Stat. 2228 (1988)(emphasis added). Concluding that "[t]he directive of the appropriations language affords us no discretion," the Commission promulgated a new rule pursuant to section 1464 prohibiting all broadcasts of indecent materials. *See Enforcement of Prohibitions Against Broadcast Obscenity and Indecency in 18 U.S.C. § 1464*, 4 FCC Rcd 457 (1988) . . . ..

A panel of this court granted petitioners' motion to stay enforcement of the ban pending judicial review, [ ]. Six months later, while briefing on the validity of the Commission's order was underway in this court, the Supreme Court issued an opinion finding a blanket ban on indecent commercial telephone message services unconstitutional. *Sable Communications of Cal., Inc. v. FCC*, 492 U.S. 115, 109 S. Ct. 2829 (1989). Believing that *Sable* left open the possibility that indecent broadcasts may be proscribed if the Commission could prove that no less restrictive measure would effectuate the government's compelling interests, the Commission sought and obtained a remand from this court in order to assemble the relevant data supporting a total ban. [ ]

The Commission subsequently solicited public comments on the validity of a total ban on broadcast indecency.   [ ]   After receiving and reviewing the comments, the Commission issued a comprehensive report concluding that "a 24-hour prohibition on indecent broadcasts comports with the constitutional standard the Supreme Court enunciated in *Sable* for the regulation of constitutionally protected speech." *Enforcement of Prohibitions Against Broadcast Indecency in 18 U.S.C. § 1464*, 5 FCC Rcd 5297, 5297 (1990). Finding a "reasonable risk that significant numbers of children ages 17 and under listen to radio and view television at all times" without "active" parental supervision, the Commission concluded that no alternative to a total ban would effectuate the government's compelling interest in protecting children from broadcast indecency. *See id.* at 5297, 5306. . . .

II.

Petitioners, an amalgam of broadcasters, industry associations, and public interest groups, present several constitutional challenges to the Commission's action. First, they claim (some more spiritedly than others) that the Commission's definition of indecency is unconstitutionally vague and overbroad. Second, they contend that a total ban on broadcast indecency cannot withstand constitutional scrutiny. We address petitioners' contentions in turn.

A.   *Vagueness and Overbreadth Challenges*

Petitioners contend that the Commission's definition of indecency--"language or material that, in context, depicts or describes, in terms patently offensive as measured by contemporary community standards for the broadcast medium, sexual or excretory activities or organs,"   [ ]--is unconstitutionally vague. A statute or regulation is void for vagueness if it "'either forbids or requires the doing of an act in terms so vague that [persons] of common intelligence must necessarily guess at its meaning and differ as to its application.'"   [ ]

We have already considered and rejected a vagueness challenge to the Commission's definition of indecency. In *ACT I*, we noted that the Supreme Court, entertaining a similar challenge in *Pacifica*, had quoted various elements of the definition with approval and had ultimately affirmed the Commission's application of the definition to the broadcast under review. *See ACT I*, 852 F.2d at 1338-39. In our view, the Supreme Court's decision in *Pacifica* dispelled any vagueness concerns attending the definition. *See id.* at 1339 . . . .. Our holding in *ACT I* precludes us from now finding the Commission's generic definition of indecency to be unconstitutionally vague.

Some of the petitioners raise the additional claim that the definition of indecency is unconstitutionally overbroad. They contend that, because the Commission fails to recognize, "serious merit" as an absolute defense to a charge of indecency, the definition sweeps even constitutionally protected expression within its ambit. [ ]

We rejected an identical overbreadth argument in *ACT I*. We noted that indecent material qualifies for First Amendment protection regardless of merit, but that even material with "significant social value" may have a strong negative impact on children. *See ACT I*, 852 F.2d at 1340. We thus found the Commission's method of identifying material suitable for broadcast only during the late night, safe harbor hours--whereby merit is treated as a "relevant factor in determining whether material is patently offensive" but "does not render such material *per se* not indecent"--to be permissible. *See id.* at 1339-40. Given that our decision today reaffirms the need for safe harbor periods during which indecent material may be broadcast and invalidates the Commission's attempt to ban such broadcasts altogether, we have no reason to revisit *ACT I*'s conclusion that the Commission's generic definition of indecency comports with constitutional overbreadth requirements.

B. *Challenge to Total Ban on Broadcast Indecency*

          . . .

We agree with petitioners that circuit precedent compels our rejection today of a total ban on the broadcast of indecent material. In *ACT I*, we stated that:

> Broadcast material that is indecent but not
> obscene is protected by the first amendment; the
> FCC may regulate such material only with due
> respect for the high value our Constitution
> places on freedom and choice of what the people
> say and hear.

852 F.2d at 1344. Addressing the scope of permissible
regulation, we explained that:

> Content-based restrictions ordinarily "may be
> sustained only if the government can show that
> the regulation is a precisely drawn means of
> serving a compelling state interest." [citation
> omitted]   The Supreme Court has recognized a
> government's interest in "safeguarding the
> physical and psychological well-being of a
> minor" as compelling." [citations omitted] But
> that interest in the context of speech control,
> may be served only by carefully-tailored
> regulation.

Id. at 1343 n.18.

We found that the Commission's elimination of the
post-10:00 p.m. "safe harbor" period failed to satisfy
these constitutional standards.   Specifically, we
concluded that:

> [T]he precision necessary to allow scope for the
> first amendment shielded freedom and choice of
> broadcasters and their audiences cannot be
> accomplished, we believe, unless the FCC adopts
> a reasonable safe harbor rule.

Id. . . .

Our holding in *ACT I* that the Commission must
identify some reasonable period of time during which
indecent material may be broadcast necessarily means
that the Commission may not ban such broadcasts
entirely. The fact that Congress itself mandated the
total ban on broadcast indecency does not alter our
view that, under *ACT I*, such a prohibition cannot
withstand constitutional scrutiny. While "we do not
ignore" Congress' apparent belief that a total ban on
broadcast indecency is constitutional, it is
ultimately the judiciary's task, particularly in the

First Amendment context, to decide whether Congress has violated the constitution. [ ] . . .

Nothing else in the intervening thirty-four months has reduced the precedential force *ACT I*. Indeed, the Supreme Court's decision in *Sable*, striking down a total ban on indecent commercial telephone messages, affirmed the protected status of indecent speech and reiterated the strict constitutional standard that government efforts to regulate the content of speech must satisfy. [ ]

Thus, neither the Commission's action prohibiting the broadcast of indecent material, nor the congressional mandate that prompted it, can pass constitutional muster under the law of this circuit.

III.

We appreciate the Commission's constraints in responding to the appropriations rider. It would be unseemly for a regulatory agency to throw down the gauntlet, even a gauntlet grounded on the Constitution, to Congress. But just as the FCC may not ignore the dictates of the legislative branch, neither may the judiciary ignore its independent duty to check the constitutional excesses of Congress. We hold that Congress' action here cannot preclude the Commission from creating a safe harbor exception to its regulation of indecent broadcasts.

Our decision today effectively returns the Commission to the position it briefly occupied after *ACT I* and prior to congressional adoption of the appropriations rider. The Commission should resume its "plans to initiate a proceeding in response to the concerns raised" in *ACT I*, which it "abandon[ed]" following Congress' mandate. [ ] We direct the Commission, in "redetermin[ing], after a full and fair hearing, . . . the times at which indecent material may be broadcast," to carefully review and address the specific concerns we raised in *ACT I*: among them, the appropriate definitions of "children" and "reasonable risk" for channeling purposes, the paucity of station- or program-specific audience data expressed as a percentage of the relevant age group population, and the scope of the government's interest in regulating indecent broadcasts. *See ACT I*, 852 F.2d at 1341-44.

For the foregoing reasons, the petition for review is granted, the order under review is vacated, and the case is remanded for further proceedings not inconsistent with this opinion.

It is so ordered.

Notes and Questions

1. The FCC has petitioned for a rehearing *en banc*. If that is not granted, the Commission is expected to seek Supreme Court review. Broadcasting, July 8, 1991 at 51.

2. If the decision is not overturned and the Commission is forced to set up a safe harbor for indecent speech, how should it go about setting the hours? What evidence will it need to support its decision?

Add to casebook p. 316, after note 4:

In *Monroe Communications*, p. 11 (this supplement), *supra*, the court of appeals held that the Commission had not adequately justified its contemporaneous complaint requirement. The FCC had argued that the rule "would guarantee the Commission flexibility in responding to the obscenity allegations in a responsible manner; would enable the Commission to put the licensee on notice that its broadcasts were unacceptable, thus minimizing the chilling effect on a broadcaster's disposition to air protected speech that might result from allowing allegations of obscenity to be raised for the first time in the context of comparative renewal hearings, and would ensure that allegations of obscenity are judged by contemporary community standards, as required by [*Miller*], rather than the standards of a later period."

The court dismissed the first argument because allegations of obscene broadcasts were clearly relevant to the public interest and no other factor bearing on the public interest was subject to a contemporaneous complaint requirement. The chilling effect argument was rejected because the court did not see how the threat of eventual nonrenewal was any more chilling than the threat of an immediate forfeiture or license revocation. Finally, the court found the argument that the requirement would ensure adherence to *Miller* to "make[] no sense whatsoever." Adjudications of obscenity, whether by the courts or the FCC, always require a determination at a later date of what the standards were at the time of the allegedly obscene broadcast. The court instructed the FCC either to consider the obscenity complaints against Video 44 or to better justify its refusal to do so.

In *Video 44*, p. 12 (this supplement), *supra*, the Commission found it unnecessary to address the obscenity complaints because it had already decided to award the license to a competing applicant.

Add to casebook p. 322, replacing Note 8:

8. During the Persian Gulf War, a St. Louis disk jockey played an old Civil Defense alert, causing listeners to believe a nuclear attack was in progress. The disk jockey was suspended, and the station issued an apology. Broadcasting, Feb. 4, 1991 at 29. The licensee was subsequently fined $25,000. Broadcasting, July 29, 1991 at 69.

9. The St. Louis incident, as well as incidents in Pasadena and Providence, have caused the head of the Mass Media Bureau to request an NPRM on hoax broadcasts. The Pasadena case involved a radio station airing a call from a man who supposedly had killed his girlfriend. A police investigation of the "murder" ensued and the hoax was only exposed when viewers of a "Unsolved Mysteries" (NBC) story on the "crime" notified police of the similarities between the caller and a disc jockey who had subsequently been hired by the station.

In the Providence hoax, a station's news director announced that the station's morning man had been shot just outside the station. The news director then refused to disclose the hoax even when ordered to by the station's general manager. The news director and morning man were both fired. Broadcasting, July 29, 1991 at 68.

<u>*Add to casebook p. 325, after 1st paragraph:*</u>

In 1990 Congress passed an exemption to the antitrust laws for "any joint discussion, consideration, review, action, or agreement by or among persons in the television industry for the purpose of, and limited to, developing and disseminating voluntary guidelines designed to alleviate the negative impact of violence in telecast material." The exemption will sunset after three years. P.L. 101-650 (1990).

<u>*Add to casebook p. 329, replacing the remainder of section D:*</u>

In July 1990 Congress passed a children's television bill limiting advertising in children's television shows and requiring the FCC to include service to children as a factor in television renewal decisions. President Bush, while expressing reservations concerning the bill's constitutionality, allowed it to become law without his signature.

The Act required the FCC to complete a proceeding implementing these requirements within 6 months. The three primary issues addressed by the proceeding were the standards to be used in setting commercial limits for children's programming, guidelines for evaluating at renewal time broadcasters' service to children, and the definition of program-length commercials.

IN THE MATTER OF POLICIES AND RULES CONCERNING CHILDREN'S TELEVISION PROGRAMMING

REVISION OF PROGRAMMING AND COMMERCIALIZATION POLICIES, ASCERTAINMENT REQUIREMENTS, AND PROGRAM LOG REQUIREMENTS FOR COMMERCIAL TELEVISION STATIONS
Federal Communications Commission, 1991.
68 R.R.2d 1615.

[For the purposes of implementing the commercial limits set forth in § 102(b) of the Act, the Commission defined children's programming as "programs originally produced and broadcast primarily for an audience of children 12 years old and under." Commercial matter was defined as "air time sold for the purposes of selling a product," but the FCC added a number of clarifications:]

5.   By requiring that air time be "sold," we mean that the advertiser must give some valuable consideration either directly or indirectly to the broadcaster or cablecaster as an inducement for airing the material. Without such a qualification, it would be difficult to distinguish mention of logos or brand name a writer or producer used to advance creative objectives. We also clarify that although our proposed definition only referred to air time sold "for purposes of selling a product," commercial matter also encompasses advertising for services.

6.   We also find that the scope of Section 317 of the Communications Act, 47 USC § 317, which governs when the sponsors of broadcast material must be identified, is not coterminous with the scope of commercial matter.   In particular we hold that material is not necessarily "commercial matter" for purposes of the Children's Television Act simply because Section 317 requires a sponsorship identification.   . . .   For example, nonprofit organizations purchasing air time for a public service message must identify themselves as sponsors under Section 317, even though such a message is not commercial material.

7.   We accordingly find that the bare sponsorship identification announcement required under Section 317 and our implementing rules, where such material is not otherwise commercial in nature, will not be deemed commercial matter under our definition here.   Thus, public service messages sponsored by nonprofit organizations that promote not-for-profit activities will not be considered commercial matter for purposes of applying the commercial limits.   Similarly, air time sold for purposes of presenting educational and informational material, including "spot" announcements, which the only sponsorship mention a "sponsored by," is not commercial matter.   The addition of product mentions or advertising to such an identification announcement, however, would constitute commercial matter. Moreover, where a station or cable operator promotes one of its upcoming programs and mentions that program's sponsor, even though not required to do so under Section 317, the mention of the sponsor will constitute commercial matter for

purposes of determining whether the commercial limits have been exceeded. In such a case, the mention of the sponsor is not required under the Rule and is thus clearly intended to promote the sponsor. Thus, if such a station or cable operator's promo (1) mentions that the upcoming program is "brought to you by" a sponsor, or (2) promotes a product or service related to the program or program sponsor, or (3) mentions a prize furnished by the program sponsor, the mention of the sponsor or the sponsor's product or services, not being required under our sponsorship identification rules, will be considered commercial matter. Promotions of upcoming programs which do not contain such sponsor-related mentions will not be deemed commercial matter.

[The Commission decided that it will count commercial minutes by the hour as opposed to by the program. Where a half-hour of children's programming is both preceded and followed by adult programming, the FCC will apply the limits on a proportionate basis. The limits will not be applied to children's programming segments less than a half hour in length.

Commercial limits will also apply to cable operators with regard to local origination channels and cable network programs. They will not, however, apply to retransmissions of broadcast channels or access channels. (These distinctions are discussed in more detail in Chapter IX).]

III. Programming Renewal Review Requirements

14. The Children's Television Act requires that, in reviewing television license renewal applications, we consider whether the licensee has served "the educational and informational needs of children through the licensee's overall programming, including programming specifically designed to serve such needs." . . . In light of the legislative intent, we will implement this programming provision by reviewing a licensee's renewal application to determine whether, over the course of its license term, it has served the educational and informational needs of children in its overall programming, including programming specifically designed to serve such needs.

A. *Age Range of "Children"*

15. The Act does not define "children" for purposes of the educational and informational programming renewal review requirement. . . . After reviewing the variety of positions taken in the record, we find that the different policies underlying the Act's programming provision necessitate a broader conception of "children" than we used for commercial limits. While it is primarily younger children who need protection from commercial matter that they do not fully comprehend, older as well as younger children have unique needs and can benefit from programming directed to them. Teenagers are undergoing a transition to adulthood. They are still very influenced by adult role models and peers, including those portrayed on television. They are generally inexperienced and yet face many crucial decisions concerning sex, drugs, and their own identities. To fully comply with the Act's directive that licensees demonstrate responsiveness to the needs of the child audience, we believe that we must interpret the programming renewal review requirement to apply to programs originally produced and broadcast for an audience of children 16 years of age and under.

. . .

18. The *Notice* asked whether the Act requires broadcasters to target particular segments of the child audience. The legislative history, we find, permits but does not require such targeting to satisfy our renewal review. Imposing such a requirement would contravene the legislative intent to afford broadcasters maximum flexibility in determining the "mix" of programming they will present to meet children's special needs. Requiring each broadcaster to serve all age groups in order to pass our renewal review would probably result in less expensive and lower quality programming, possibly engendering what INTV describes as "sameness and mediocrity." We thus decline to adopt suggestions that broadcasters program to all ages or to each subset of children within the under 16 range. Stations may select the age groups they can most effectively serve.

B. Standard

　　1.　Programming

19.　Although we stated the desire to avoid any *de facto* system of "precensorship" and to leave it to licensees to interpret the meaning of educational and informational programming, the *Notice* asked those commenters desiring a delineation of the Act's programming renewal review requirement to address what definition of "educational and informational" programming we might use.　The *Notice* specifically referred to a description by Senator Inouye, as programming which furthers a child's intellectual, emotional and social development.　After further reflection, we believe that a general definition of "educational and informational" programming for children would provide needed guidance to the industry as well as to Commission staff administering the statute, and would give licensees sufficient flexibility to exercise their discretion in serving children's needs.　We also encourage licensees to use the assessment criteria proposed in the *Notice* in determining how to meet the educational and informational needs of children in their communities.

.　.　.

21.　We believe that a definition based on Senator Inouye's view, described above, or based on McGannon's formulation--content that serves children's cognitive/intellectual or social/emotional needs--is closer to the spirit of the Act and to our desire to stimulate, and not dictate, programming responsive to children's needs. Thus, programming that furthers the positive development of the child in any respect, including the child's cognitive/intellectual or emotional/social needs, can contribute to satisfying the licensee's obligation to serve the educational and informational needs of children.

22.　The *Notice* proposed to require each licensee to assess the needs of children given (1) the circumstances within the community, (2) other programming on the station, (3) programming aired on other broadcast stations within the community, and (4) other programs for children available in the broadcaster's community of license.　Licensees would then air programs intended to meet "the educational and informational needs of children" responding to this assessment.   In order to avoid unnecessary burdens, we are not requiring use of the proposed assessment criteria.   We do, however, adopt them as permissive guidelines for exercise of licensee discretion in applying this definition. These factors can serve to make licensees' decisionmaking process more objective and may make it easier for licensees to justify programming decisions that are questioned. We therefore encourage their use. We are concerned with licensee responsiveness to children's needs, not with the precise methodology they use to assess those needs.   We thus do not adopt proposals for structured assessment procedures.   Licensees will retain reasonable discretion to determine the manner in which they assess the educational and informational needs of children in their communities, provided that they are able to demonstrate the methodology they have used.

. . .

24. The Act imposes no quantitative standards and the legislative history suggests that Congress meant that no minimum amount criterion be imposed.   Given this strong legislative directive direction, and the latitude afforded broadcasters in fulfilling the programming requirement, we believe that the amount of "specifically designed" programming necessary to comply with the Act's requirement is likely to vary according to other circumstances, including but not limited to, type of programming aired and other nonbroadcast efforts made by the station.   We thus decline to establish any minimum programming requirement for licensees for renewal review independent of that established in the Act.

25. At the request of numerous parties, we clarify that short segment programming, including vignettes and PSAs, may qualify as specifically designed educational and informational programming for children. Such material is well suited to children's short attention spans and can often be locally produced with acceptable production quality. It thus may be a particularly appropriate way for a local broadcaster to respond to specific children's concerns. Whether or not short segment programming fully satisfies the requirement to air programming

"specifically designed" to meet children's needs depends on the entire context of the licensee's programming and nonbroadcast efforts directed at children. We also clarify that qualifying programming need not be locally produced and need not be live action, as opposed to animation. We can see no reason in the statute's purpose or legislative history for these restrictions. As the legislative history also indicates, general audience programming can contribute, as part of the licensee's overall programming, to serving children's needs pursuant to the Act. It does not by definition, however, satisfy the additional requirement that licensees air some programming "specifically designed" to serve the educational and informational needs of children.

. . .

2.   Nonbroadcast efforts

27.   Section 103 (b) of the Act permits the Commission, in evaluating compliance with the broadcaster's obligation to demonstrate at renewal time that it served the educational and informational needs of children, to consider "in addition" to its programming (1) "any special nonbroadcast efforts . . . which enhance the educational and informational value" of programming meeting such needs and (2) any "special efforts" to produce or support programming broadcast by another station in the licensee's market that is specifically designed to meet such needs.
. . .

28.   For nonbroadcast efforts to contribute to satisfying the Act's programming renewal review requirement, they must enhance the "educational and informational value" to children of television programming broadcast either by the licensee or by another station in the community. Thus, however, praiseworthy, community outreach efforts unrelated to television programming will not qualify. Similarly, we do not believe that support for children's radio programming, as some urge, although a very laudable objective, qualifies under Section 103(b)(2) as support for another licensee's programming. . . .
For efforts to be credited toward satisfying the Act's programming renewal review requirements, they must

somehow   enhance   or   support   educational   and
informational television programming for children.

26. If a station produces or buys children's programs
broadcast on another station, so as to qualify under
Section 103(b)(2) of the Act, we hold that both
stations may rely on such programming in their renewal
applications. The extent of support, measured in both
time and money, given to another station's programming
will determine the weight afforded it. . . .

. . .

V. Program-Length Children's Commercials

A. Definition

40.   We find that the definition of program-length
children's commercial proposed in the *Notice*--a
program associated with a product in which commercials
for that product aired--strikes the best balance
between the important interests involved.   This
definition protects children from the confusion and
deception the intermixture of related program and
commercial material may inflict upon them, and still
preserves the creative freedom and practical revenue
sources that make children's programming possible.
For the reasons given below, we adopt this definition.

41.   ACT maintains . . . that the Commission should
establish a rebuttable presumption that if there is
less   than   a   two-year   time   span   between   the
introduction of a television program and a related
product or *vice versa*, this is *prima facie* evidence
that the show is a program-length commercial. We do
not find that this is a viable definition. We agree
with numerous commenters that it would jeopardize
highly acclaimed children's shows such as Sesame
Street   and   Disney   programs   that   have   products
associated with them. As CTW, the producer of Sesame
Street, states, a program's relationship to products
is not necessarily indicative of commercial content.
According to CTW, ACT's proposal would inhibit the
simultaneous introduction of any new CTW program
series   and   associated   products,   such   as   books,
magazines, games and computer software whose purpose
is to extend the educational benefits of the series.
We fear that such a definition would stifle creativity

by restricting the sources that writers could draw
upon for characters, would limit revenues from
merchandising which are an important source of
production funding, and would ignore the educational
role toys or other related products can play in child
development.

. . .

44.   The definition of children's program-length
commercial that we are now adopting--a program
associated with a product, in which commercials for
that product are aired--is clear, easy to understand
and apply, and narrowly tailored.   It directly
addresses a fundamental regulatory concern, that
children who have difficulty enough distinguishing
program content from unrelated commercial matter, not
be all the more confused by a show that interweaves
program content and commercial matter.   Removal of
related commercial matter should help alleviate this
confusion.   Our definition also would cover programs
in which a product or service is advertised within the
body of the program and not separated from program
content as children's commercials are required to be.
Contrary to ACT's view, we find that our definition
clarifies the manner in which our traditional
definition of program-length commercial applies to
children's programs.   We have previously so held.
Given the First Amendment context of this issue, our
approach is a restrained one.   Should abuses occur,
however, we will not hesitate to revisit this issue.
We also note that our definition harmonizes with, and
codifies to some degree, existing policies with
respect to host-selling and adequate separation of
commercial from program material in children's
programs.[147]

---

147.   Our policy against "host-selling" prohibits
the use of program talent to deliver commercials.
Action for Children's Television, 50 FCC2d 1, 8, 16-17
(1974). The policy applies to endorsements or selling
by animated cartoon characters as well as "live"
program hosts.   [ ]   "Host-selling" is a special
application of our more general policy with respect to
separation of commercial and program material.   The
separation policy is an attempt to aid children in
distinguishing advertising from program material.   It

45.   In addition, a program will be considered a
program-length commercial if a product associated with
the program appears in commercial spots not separated
from the start or close of the program by at least 60
seconds of unrelated material.   It is reasonably
likely that a young viewer will tune in immediately
before or stay tuned immediately after a program, and
that in such circumstances an adjacent spot would have
the same effect as if the spot were included in the
program itself.   We do not find record evidence
justifying extending this Rule beyond 60 seconds, or
further expanding our host-selling policy, as ACT
requests.   In light of the short attention spans of
children, particularly younger children most likely to
confuse program and commercial material, we believe
that a 60-second separation is adequate.

. . .

Notes and Questions

1.   The new Commission rules governing children's
television are scheduled to become effective Oct. 1,
1991.   The first renewal applications that will be
evaluated under the new criteria will be those due to
be filed Feb. 1, 1992.

2.   In an omitted portion of *Children's Television
Programming*, the FCC denied ACT's petition regarding
interactive children's programs, p. 329 (the
casebook), *supra*, on the ground that there was no
evidence that any interactive toys were currently for
sale.

Add to casebook p. 331, replacing 6th full paragraph:

A lottery is defined as anything containing three
elements: chance, consideration and a prize. If all
three are present, the broadcaster cannot air any
information either as an advertisement or public

---

requires that broadcasters separate the two types of
content by use of special measures such as "bumpers"
(*e.g.*, "And now its time for a commercial break."
"And now back to the [title of the program]"). Action
for Children's Television, 50 FCC2d at 14-16. . . .

service announcement concerning the lottery, and even news coverage is limited to situations where the lottery is truly newsworthy.

Until recently it was irrelevant whether the beneficiary of the lottery was a commercial enterprise or a non-profit one. This was changed by the Charity Games Advertising Clarification Act of 1988, which expanded the exceptions to § 1304, effective May 7, 1990. The Commission also amended its rules to conform to these changes. Broadcasters may now advertise lotteries "if they are conducted by: (a) not-for-profit organizations; (b) governmental organizations; or (c) commercial entities, provided the lottery is clearly occasional and ancillary to the primary business of the commercial organization." Broadcast of Lottery Information (Charity Games), 67 R.R.2d 996 (1990). However, state law has not been preempted, leaving states free to restrict or prohibit lottery advertising. Thus, in many states the restrictions on broadcasters have effectively remained unchanged.

Add to casebook p. 334, replacing 2nd full paragraph:

Recently, a district court declared the adjacent state restriction unconstitutional as applied to a North Carolina radio station. The station, located near the Virginia border, sought a declaratory judgment so that it could accept advertising for the Virginia State Lottery.

The court found that the application of the restriction to the station failed the third part of the *Central Hudson* test. Because the vast majority of the station's listeners were in Virginia and those listeners in Virginia were heavily exposed to Virginia broadcast stations--for whom the lottery advertising was legal--the court found that prohibiting the radio station from broadcasting lottery advertising failed "materially to protect North Carolina residents from the harms which may result from lottery advertising." Edge Broadcasting Co. v. United States, 732 F.Supp. 633, 67 R.R.2d 981 (E.D.Va.1990)

Under the Charity Games Advertising Clarification Act of 1988, p. 331 (the casebook), *supra*, the adjacent states restriction was eliminated for states that have state-run lotteries. Regardless of whether a state has a state-run lottery, it does not apply to lotteries run by other government organizations or by non-profit or commercial organizations.

Chapter VIII

NONCOMMERCIAL BROADCASTING

There are no additions to Chapter VIII.

Chapter IX

CABLE TELEVISION

Add to casebook p. 406, after 1st paragraph:

4. The 1984 Act Reconsidered

As part of the 1984 Act, the FCC was required to conduct a study of the cable industry's operation under the Act and to submit a report to Congress based on that report. The report was to be submitted no later than Oct. 28, 1990. In accordance with that requirement, the FCC issued an NOI in December 1989 seeking comment on the validity of various allegations that the industry was abusing its market power.

There are increasing consumer complaints about high and rising basic cable rates, poor service quality, and the dropping or repositioning of broadcast signals. Television broadcasters echo the last complaint and have also voiced concern about cable operators' ability to offer their own basic channels that compete unfairly with broadcasters for local advertising revenue. Other video service competitors--such as multichannel multipoint distribution service ("MMDS") companies and distributors of programming to home satellite dish ("HSD") owners--allege that large, vertically integrated cable operators are denying them access to programs. Some program suppliers assert that they cannot gain access to the cable systems of operators that also produce their own programming. Some program suppliers also complain that rising national concentration in cable system ownership has led to their inability to gain access to large cable systems. Operators of small, independent cable systems and non-cable multichannel video services alike claim that they pay discriminatorily high rates to certain program sources which are under the control or strong influence of large multiple system operators ("MSOs"). The common thread running through all these complaints is that, with the advent of large, multi-system cable owners and their growing control over sources of programming, the cable industry has become so concentrated that it is no longer responsive to the public and can now unfairly impede competitors from offering alternative service to viewers.

Competition, Rate Regulation and the Commission's Policies Relating to the Provision of Cable Television Service, 55 Fed.Reg. 1484 (Dec. 29, 1989).

The complaints noted in the Commission's NOI had already led to a number of proposals to reregulate the cable industry. Several bills to amend the Communications Act to increase regulatory control of cable were introduced in the House and Senate. Provisions in these bills covered everything from expanded rate regulation, to must-carry rules (see discussion, *infra*), to permitting the telephone companies to provide cable service.

In July 1990 the Commission concluded its inquiry by adopting the report required by the 1984 Act. It found numerous problems with the cable industry including vertically integrated cable programmers that denied programming to cable competitors, cable operators that denied programming services carriage, municipal franchise requirements that prohibited competition, and "a general pattern of problems with cable technical quality and customer service has emerged." Other FCC findings were that the compulsory copyright license for cable (discussed later in this chapter) constituted an unfair subsidy and that the 1984 Act's enforcement provisions for leased access channels were ineffective.

The report concluded that the primary cause of the problems noted in the NOI is the lack of competition for cable. The Commission's suggested solution therefore would be to have Congress pass legislation aimed at promoting competition from other "multichannel video providers" such as direct broadcast satellites and MMDS. (These technologies are discussed in Chapter X). The Commission also recommended limiting the ability of municipalities to restrict the number of cable franchisees in a given area.

Other recommendations contained in the report included a Congressionally enacted must-carry rule or, in its absence, repeal of the compulsory copyright license, as well as a prohibition on cable operators demanding financial interests or exclusivity from independent programming services in return for carriage. Broadcasting, July 30, 1990 at 27.

In 1991 the Commission changed its definition of effective competition in order to increase the number of cable systems subject to rate regulation. Effective competition is now defined as either six broadcast channels available in the community or a competing multichannel video provider that reaches at least half the market and serves a minimum of 10 percent of its homes.

The exact impact of the new definition is not yet clear. NCTA has indicated that 61 percent of the cable systems in the country serving 34 percent of the subscribers would be subject to rate regulation. However, NTIA placed the figures at 52 percent of the systems and 18 percent of the subscribers. Broadcasting, June 17, 1991 at 20.

Regardless, several Congressional leaders indicated that the FCC had not gone far enough and that they would continue to push for additional cable legislation. Although the exact form of legislation they are seeking is not yet known, it will probably be similar to the bill approved last year by the House Commerce Committee. The bill would have authorized the FCC to regulate rates for retransmission of broadcast channels, establish technical, consumer protection and customer service standards, and set maximum rates for leased access channels. The bill would also have required cable operators to devote 25 percent of their channel capacity to retransmission of broadcast channels. Vertically integrated programmers would not have been allowed to unreasonably deny access to multichannel video systems. Finally, a three-year restriction on the sale of newly acquired franchises would have been imposed. Broadcasting, July 30, 1990 at 29.

Add to casebook p. 412, after note 5:

5a. In Chicago Cable Communications v. Chicago Cable
Commission, 879 F.2d 1540, 66 R.R.2d 1222 (7th
Cir.1989), cert. petition pending, the Commission
fined a group of three cable franchisees for failing
to honor the local origination clause of the
franchises. That clause required 4 1/2 hours per week
of local programming geared to Chicago. The violation
was said to have occurred when the group presented
local programming that had been prepared by a suburban
affiliate even though the group said that it selected
programs that it believed would be interesting to its
Chicago customers.

Among other defenses, the group contended that
the First Amendment prevented the content control
inherent in the clause and its enforcement. The
district court enforced the fine, and the court of
appeals affirmed. The court adhered to an earlier
cable decision in which it said that "there are enough
differences between cable television and the non-
television media to allow more government regulation
of the former." In deciding to adopt the *O'Brien*
analysis, the court said that it was not abandoning
First Amendment scrutiny because of the natural
monopoly characteristics of cable. "Rather, each
medium of expression must be assessed by standards
properly suited to it."

The court concluded that the government had met
its burdens of establishing the elements of the
O'Brien test. Promotion of "community self-expression
can increase direct communications between residents
by featuring topics of local concern. Encouragement
of 'localism' certainly qualifies as an important or
substantial interest." The court approvingly quoted
the district court's statement that the "important
qualities of localism (community pride, cultural
diversity, *etc.*) may not be furthered enough simply by
the availability of local broadcast television
stations for retransmission over cable systems, but
may require original cable programming specifically
concerning the locality and directed at that
locality's residents." An additional interest
fostered by the requirement was providing jobs for
residents: "Production of programming in the City
provides career opportunities as well as potential

internships for students studying communications at local schools." These were enough to satisfy *O'Brien*'s second prong.

As to the congruence between means and ends, the court relied on Supreme Court language to the effect that "so long as the neutral regulation promotes a substantial government interest that would be achieved less effectively absent the regulation," an incidental burden on speech is permissible. Here on the one hand was a requirement of only 4 1/2 hours per week with no requirement of any specific kind of programming. "As long as the particular episode is geared to Chicago-- be it sports, politics, news, weather, entertainment, *etc.*--[the group] has full discretion over what it may desire to transmit. This restriction on [the group's] control in meeting the minimal [local origination] requirements does not divest it of discretion, for, as in *Midwest Video*, the cable operator here still retains the ultimate decision" over which programs to present.

On the other hand, cable "is an economically scarce medium. Unlike the traditional forms of print media, a cable programmer enjoys a virtual monopoly over its area, without the threat of an alternative provider. As a result the government, which serves as the representative of the cable customers, is duty- bound to recognize the effects of 'medium scarcity' by ensuring that the few programmers who are granted a franchise make optimum use of it. [ ] With this in mind, it is within the City's rights, arguably its responsibilities, to proffer some requirements guaranteeing that the cable customers are, to the extent possible, accorded a range of programming from the franchisee, since the cable viewing public has no other channel to which to turn."

Add to casebook p. 414, after note 9:

9a. In early 1990 in the *Preferred* remand, the district court ruled on a number of motions for summary judgment by both parties. In making the rulings the court divided the various franchise requirement into two categories: restrictions imposing an incidental burden on speech, which are subject to the *O'Brien* test, and restrictions "intended to curtail expression," which are subject to the highest level of judicial scrutiny. The court defined this to mean that the government had to show that the challenged regulation "is a precisely drawn means of serving a compelling state interest."

The court held that the limit of one cable operator in any franchise area was an incidental burden. Nevertheless, it was unconstitutional as a matter of law because the one operator requirement was too restrictive a method of achieving the city's substantial interests in minimizing disruption and visual blight.

A requirement of participation of local individuals and/or groups in the ownership and operation of the cable system was held non-incidental "as it, at the very least, indirectly bans speech by favoring speakers 'responsive to the needs of the South Central area residents' over others." The court then found the government's interest in localism compelling, and thus the requirement was held constitutional.

Mandatory access channels were also held a non-incidental burden on speech. The city asserted two compelling interests in access channels: "(1) to protect the First Amendment interests of various parties by promoting the availability of diverse sources of information over a cable system; and (2) providing groups and individuals historically excluded from the electronic media with access to the medium of cable communications."

Although these were held to be compelling interests, the requirement was still found unconstitutional. The reason was that the city failed to explain why eight channels were necessary to achieve these interests.

The court also found unconstitutional the city's use of overall character as a factor in awarding a cable franchise. Because the character inquiry was not limited to past criminal or civil liability, but in fact included consideration of whether the applicant had ever "initiated litigation against a franchising authority or ha[d] a franchising authority instigated litigation against it," the court found the

requirement a non-incidental burden on speech. The
requirement was not narrowly tailored to serve the
city's asserted interest in protecting its citizens
from fraud because it allowed the city to take into
account whether the applicant had ever brought
"legitimate challenges to franchise ordinances
invoking first amendment rights."

The state-of-the-art-technology requirement was
also found a non-incidental burden on speech after the
city asserted as one of its purposes "promoting
universal availability of educational opportunities."
The promotion of certain forms of speech over others,
here educational speech, made the requirement non-
incidental. Because the city failed to support its
conclusion that this requirement would promote its
interests with empirical evidence, the court found
that they were not compelling interests.

The court also found provisions allowing the city
to purchase the franchise at below-market value and to
require continued service after the expiration or
revocation of the franchise unconstitutional under
O'Brien. Again applying *O'Brien*, it upheld provisions
prohibiting transfer of the franchise without the
city's consent and requiring universal service.
Finally, it struck down a five-year franchise term
because the city failed to offer evidence why such a
short franchise term was needed. Preferred
Communications, Inc. v. City of Los Angeles, 67 R.R.2d
366 (CD Cal990).

6b.   A few months later, the court issued still
another series of rulings on motions for summary
judgment. Among the more important of these were the
following: The five percent franchise fee was held to
be an incidental burden on speech. The court further
held that the fee furthered the substantial government
interest "in receiving compensation from private
individuals who benefit from the commercial
exploitation of that property" in a narrowly tailored
fashion. Thus, under *O'Brien*, the fee requirement is
constitutional.

However, the Court found the city's requirement
of a $10,000 filing fee, a $500 good faith deposit and
a $60,000 processing fee (this last fee to be paid
only by the winning applicant) to be unconstitutional.

The city had justified these fees as necessary to cover the costs of the franchising process. Because the fees were calculated to cover the original franchising process, some of which had subsequently been declared unconstitutional, the city was, in effect, requiring the applicants to pay for the expenses of an unconstitutional review process.

A requirement that the cable operator provide "public access production facilities, equipment and staff available for noncommercial programming purposes" was found unconstitutional because the city's answer and subsequent briefs did not address the allegations in Preferred's complaint regarding this issue even though the city had the burden of proving the requirement's constitutionality. More specific equipment requirements were struck down because the city's asserted interest was to further the development of PEG programs and the court had already found the PEG requirement unconstitutional.

Finally, a requirement that the cable franchisee create a cable advisory board, every aspect of which would be subject to the city's approval, was found unconstitutional. The city justified the board as a means of furthering localism. Finding that the board constituted a direct burden on speech, the court held that, to be constitutional, it had to be a precisely drawn means of furthering the compelling localism interests. Because there was nothing in the requirement limiting the board's role to advising the cable company on local interests, the requirement, in the court's opinion, was not precisely drawn and, thus, unconstitutional. Preferred Communications, Inc. v. City of Los Angeles, 68 R.R.2d 121 (CD Cal990).

Add to casebook p. 416, after 3rd full paragraph:

As a result of the FCC's adoption of new syndication exclusivity rules, p. 430 (the casebook), *infra*, the CRT drastically reduced the application of the syndex surcharge. Essentially, it applies only to retransmission of stations that were covered by the old rules but not the new ones. Broadcasting, July 23, 1990 at 80.

Add to casebook p. 430, after 4th full paragraph:

Various cable companies and satellite retransmitters appealed.

UNITED VIDEO, INC. v. FEDERAL COMMUNICATIONS COMMISSION
United States Court of Appeals, District of Columbia Circuit, 1989.
___ F.2d ___ , 66 R.R.2d 1865.

Before WALD, CHIEF JUDGE, and EDWARDS and SILBERMAN, CIRCUIT JUDGES

WALD, CHIEF JUDGE:

A syndicated television program is a program marketed from its supplier to local television stations by means other than a television network. In 1988, the FCC reinstated its "syndicated exclusivity" rules. These rules allow the supplier of a syndicated program to agree with a broadcast television station that the station shall be the exclusive presenter of the program in its local broadcast area. A broadcast station with exclusive rights to a syndicated program can forbid any cable television station from importing the program into its local broadcast area from a distant station.

Petitioners, mostly cable television companies whose distant signal offerings will be restricted under the new rules, challenge the rules as arbitrary and capricious, and as violative of the Copyright Act of 1976, the Cable Act of 1984, and the First Amendment. We find that the Commission's action is within its authority and is not arbitrary and capricious. Accordingly we deny the petition for review.

I. Background

This Court has had several opportunities to examine the checkered history of the regulation of cable television by the Federal Communications Commission . . .. *See e.g.,* [*Century Communications*]; [*Quincy Cable*]; [*Home Box Office*]. As a prelude to our analysis in this case, we review briefly highlights from the history of syndicated exclusivity regulation ("syndex").

The volatile relationship between cable and broadcast television has traditionally hinged on the ability of cable television stations to receive the signal that a broadcast station sends over the air, and to retransmit that signal to subscribers via a cable. This retransmission is not a "broadcast," for it is not a dissemination of radio communications intended to be received by the public. [ ] The Communications Act forbids a broadcast station from rebroadcasting another broadcast station's signal without permission, 47 USC § 325(a), but does not forbid cable retransmission.

Prior to the 1976 revision of the copyright laws, two Supreme Court decisions held that the distinction between broadcasting and cable transmission had important copyright law implications. [*Fortnightly*] held that when a cable company posted an antenna high on a hilltop, and ran a cable from the antenna into its subscribers' homes, it did nothing significantly different than an individual television owner does when she puts an antenna on her own roof, and runs a cable from it to her television inside. In particular, the cable company's retransmission was not a "performance" of the television program, and so did not violate the copyright on it. [*Teleprompter*] extended this reasoning to cases where the cable brought a program to a distant market. Accordingly, cable companies were free, as far as copyright law was concerned, to pick up signals aired by broadcasters and retransmit them throughout the country.

The distress felt by originating broadcasters whose signals were retransmitted in this way was matched only by the anger of local broadcasters in the receiving end communities, who watched the cable companies importing into their local markets the very programs that they were themselves showing, and to which they had purchased exclusive broadcast rights. [ ] Even before the *Fortnightly* decision validated this practice against copyright claims, the FCC decided that it was an unfair form of competition. Beginning in 1965, the Commission promulgated exclusivity rules that protected local broadcasters from the importation into their markets of distant signals that duplicated signals to which they had purchased exclusive rights. [ ] These rules provided nonduplication protection for both network and syndicated programs. In 1966, the Commission expanded the rules . . . and required all cable systems to notify the Commission before carrying any distant signal. [ ]

The Commission for some time attempted to review every importation of a distant signal into any of the top one hundred local television markets for consistency with "the establishment and healthy maintenance of television broadcast service in the area." [ ] This proved to be an administrative impossibility, however, and the Commission sought a more workable scheme. In 1972, the Commission adopted an industry "consensus agreement," that provided comprehensive regulation of the relationship between broadcast and cable television. [ ] The consensus agreement included syndex rules. [ ]

In 1976, Congress finally got around to addressing the question of the copyright liability of cable companies that carried distant signals. Congress provided, in the Copyright Revision Act of 1976, a compulsory licensing scheme whereby cable companies paid an administratively-set fee for such carriage. Subsequently, in 1980, the FCC decided that, given the new copyright regime, syndex protection was no longer in the public interest, although network exclusivity was retained. [ ] The Commission stated that the elimination of syndex would cause no significant harm to broadcast stations.

Broadcast stations petitioned the Commission for a reconsideration of its negative position on syndex in 1984, but the Commission refused to budge, saying that there had been no change in circumstances that would justify a change in its position. [ ] In 1987, however, the Commission began another review of its 1980 decision to eliminate syndex, and in 1988 it promulgated the rules challenged in this case. *In the Matter of Amendment of Parts 73 and 76 of the Commission's Rules Relating to Program Exclusivity in the Cable and Broadcast Industries,* 3 F.C.C.Rcd. 5299 [64 R.R.2d 1818] (1988), *on reh'g,* 4 F.C.C.Rcd. 2711 [66 R.R.2d 44] (1989) (rules codified at 47 C.F.R. §§73.658, 76.92-76.97, 76.151-76.163). The Commission decided that its 1980 decision reflected an imperfect understanding of the role cable was to assume in the ensuing decade as a full competitor to broadcast television.   The Commission found that with the enormous growth in cable's audience and advertising revenues, the lack of syndex was harming broadcast stations, and might have been significantly affecting the supply of syndicated programs.   The Commission decided to reinstate syndex in view of the changes in the cable television industry that occurred between 1980 and 1988.

II. Arbitrariness and Caprice

A. *The Commission's Factual Findings*

The Commission's decision to reinstate syndex rests on its finding that syndex rules will promote diversity in syndicated programming.   In the report accompanying the rules, the Commission found that unrestricted importation of distant signals (*i.e.*, no syndex protection) leads to duplication of programming in local broadcasting areas; this duplication lessens the value of syndicated programs to broadcast stations; that loss of value in turn lowers the price syndicated program suppliers will receive for their programs; and all of this ultimately reduces the incentive for syndicated program suppliers to produce programs, which translates into a reduction in the diversity of programming available to the public. [ ] On the basis of this scenario the Commission concluded that syndex rules should be reinstated in order to promote diversity of programming.

The petitioners challenge the FCC's rule as arbitrary and capricious, for want of support in the rulemaking record.   Our review on such a claim is narrow: the court must not substitute its judgment for that of the agency, but it must ensure that the agency has examined the relevant data and articulated a satisfactory explanation for its action, including a "rational connection between the facts found and the choice made."   [ ]   Since this action represents a change in agency policy, the court must also ensure that the agency supplied a "reasoned analysis indicating that its prior policies and standards are being deliberately changed, not casually ignored." [ ]   We will examine each of the links in the Commission's alleged causal chain.

1. Duplication

The petitioners do not challenge the Commission's finding that unrestricted importation of distant signals leads to duplication of programming between broadcast and cable channels. . . .

2. Lessening of Value of Syndicated Programs to Local Broadcast Stations

The petitioners hotly contest the Commission's finding that program duplication lessens the value of syndicated programs purchased by local broadcast stations. However, the Commission's report cites substantial evidence from which it could reasonably draw this conclusion. The Commission discusses two related ways in which duplication lessens the value of syndicated programs: audience diversion and the loss of exclusivity as a competitive tool.

The Commission found that duplication of programming diverts a substantial portion of the broadcast audience to cable. The evidence was strongest regarding diversion caused by a cable station's *simultaneous* transmission of a program being aired by a broadcast channel, for such diversion can be gauged by ratings information. . . .

The Commission reasonably inferred that diversion lessened the value of the programming by lowering advertising revenues. The petitioners contest this finding, claiming it is based on a single study, which they attack as faulty. However, the report makes clear that the Commission relied on the study for only a rough approximation of the decrease in advertising revenue. More important was the hardly controversial conclusion that the amount that advertisers will pay depends on the size of the audience that a program attracts. [ ] This statement needs no detailed study to support it.

. . .

The Commission's report does not specify quite so clearly how it reached the conclusion that *non-simultaneous* transmission of duplicative programming (including transmission of different episodes of the same program) also causes audience diversion. The one sentence explicitly devoted to this question in the report says that "the quantity of non-simultaneous duplication documented in the record in this proceeding, taken as a whole, presents compelling evidence that substantial diversion is taking place." [ ]   This sentence suggests that the Commission has simply assumed diversion from the conceded fact of non-simultaneous duplication. The Commission points to no specific empirical support for this statement in the record.

While it is intuitively reasonable to assume that simultaneous duplication causes diversion, the question of non-simultaneous duplication seems more varied and complex. . . . If the Commission had relied solely on its assumption of audience diversion as evidence that non-simultaneous duplication lessens the value of programs to broadcast stations, we might well have felt obliged to require some supplementation or further explanation of its reasoning.

However, the Commission relies on more solid evidence that duplication makes programming less valuable. The evidence is that all stations, broadcast and cable, want exclusivity. . . . The reason, as the FCC notes in its report, is that exclusivity gives stations the opportunity to promote themselves as the only presenter of a certain program. If a broadcaster spends money promoting a duplicated program, some of the value of the expenditure will be captured by the cable company that is importing the same program. Syndex will give the local broadcaster a competitive tool that it can use both to call attention to the particular program and to "alert viewers to the general attractiveness of the broadcaster's whole range of programming." [ ] The strong desire of all stations for complete exclusivity is evidence that even non-simultaneous duplication lessens the value of programming, whether because of audience diversion or for other reasons.

While the Commission's report may leave something to be desired in its detail on the dangers of non-simultaneous duplication, we do not think its conclusion that even this type of duplication lessens the value of programming for broadcast stations can be called arbitrary or capricious. The record as a whole shows that both broadcast and cable companies want complete exclusivity; the Commission did not act without reason in concluding that exclusivity must be a valuable commodity, and conversely that lack of exclusivity diminishes the value of a program.

B. Effects on Program Supply

The weakest link in the FCC's causal chain is its claim that reinstating syndex will affect the supply of syndicated programming. And indeed, throughout the rule making proceeding, the Commission has always conceded that there is no direct, empirical evidence that syndex will actually increase program diversity, explaining that such evidence would be particularly difficult to obtain empirically. [ ]

We do not think that the absence of empirical evidence is fatal to the Commission's claim. Courts reviewing an agency's selection of means to accomplish policy goals are "not entitled to insist on empirical data for every proposition on which the selection depends." [ ] In [*Century Communications*], which struck down the FCC's must-carry regulations, this Court noted that an agency contention may be "so obvious or commonsensical that it needs no empirical support to stand up." [ ]

We think the Commission's conclusion about the link between lack of program diversity and lowered broadcast revenues due to lack of exclusivity is sufficiently in accord with accepted economic theory that it can stand without empirical support, particularly since we agree with the Commission that it would be very difficult for it to show the degree to which programs are currently *not* being produced because of the lack of syndex protection. . . . [T]he FCC has assumed only that increasing the value of programs to broadcast companies will increase the amount paid for them, and that these higher prices will improve product supply. The Commission explains that "[p]rogram suppliers, like other business people, respond to incentives. . . . Incentives to develop new programs are greatest when program suppliers are able to sell their programs wherever there are viewers (or advertisers) willing to pay for them." [ ] These claims, unlike the ones made by the FCC in *Century Communications*, do not "beg[] incredulity," 835 F.2d at 302; rather they are reasonable.

. . .

Having tested each link in the Commission's causal chain, we find that it used valid reasoning to conclude that syndex rules will increase the diversity of programming options available to the public. Its imposition of syndex was adequately supported by the rulemaking record.

C. Change in Agency Course

The petitioners complain that the Commission has not adequately explained why it is reinstating syndex rules only eight years after abandoning them, and only four years after reaffirming its decision to abandon them. However, the Commission's report, which examines in great detail its 1980 decision to eliminate syndex, meets this circuit's standard that an agency changing course must "supply a reasoned analysis indicating that its prior policies and standards are being deliberately changed, not casually ignored." [*Action for Children's Television*]

The Commission's report reviews in detail the history of the regulation of cable, including, in particular, the 1980 decision to eliminate syndex rules. [ ] The report notes several ways in which the Commission now feels the 1980 decision to have been inadequate. First, the report discusses how circumstances have changed since 1980. The principal change has been the unforeseen emergence of cable television as a full competitor to broadcast television. As the report documents, cable's audience and advertising revenues have increased dramatically and unexpectedly since 1980. In 1980, cable served 19% of television households, but in 1988 it served 51%, a percentage the FCC projected would rise to 60% by 1996. [ ] In 1980, the Commission had predicted that cable penetration would never go beyond 48%. [ ] Cable advertising revenues were $45.5 million in 1980, but they grew to over $1 billion in 1908; cable's share of total television advertising revenue climbed from less than 0.5% to more than 6%. [ ] This unexpected growth, the Commission notes, substantially undermines its 1980 findings that repeal of syndex would not cause significant audience diversion or otherwise harm broadcast stations.

The Commission also faults its earlier studies for focusing on the effects repeal of syndex would have on individual stations, rather than its effects on the competitive process and the incentive for production of new programs. . . .

          . . .

The Commission in its report also acknowledges that the absence of syndex provides consumers with the benefit of "time and episode diversity." A cable station, free of syndex restraints, may import a different episode of a program than the one aired by a broadcast station, or the same episode at a different time of day. The Commission suggests, however, that this diversity must be balanced against the lack of diversity engendered by duplication, and by the reduced incentive for the production of new programs. The Commission also suggests that market forces will allow duplication where viewers value it sufficiently, since stations with exclusive rights to a program can always sell the right to duplicate it. Finally, the Commission notes that the value of cable in providing time diversity has been lessened by the significant increase in the penetration of video cassette recorders (up from 1.5% of television households in 1979 to 58.1% today), since VCRs allow viewers to provide time diversity for themselves. [ ]

The Commission's report *in toto* suggests it undertook a thoroughgoing review of the syndex question and came to a new result with full awareness of its prior choices. . . . Accordingly, we reject the petitioners' claim that the Commission's rules are arbitrary and capricious.

III. The Commission's Authority

[Petitioners also argued that the syndex rules were an attempt to impose copyright liability and as such preempted by the Copyright Act of 1976. The court rejected this argument relying on both the text and legislative history of the Copyright Act as well as the fact that the previous syndex rules were in effect when the 1976 Act was passed.]

B. The Cable Act

The Cable Communications Policy Act of 1984 amended the Communications Act to explicitly grant the FCC a power it had previously only inferred from its general authority to regulate television: the power to regulate cable television. [ ] However, the Act also set some limits on that power, and in particular it provided:

(1) Any Federal agency, State, or franchising authority may not impose requirements regarding the provision or content of cable television services, except as expressly provided in this subchapter.

. . .

47 U.S.C. § 544(f). The petitioners claim that this section forbids syndex rules.

The Commission argues that the legislative history of Section 544(f) shows that the term "requirements," as used in the section, refers only to *affirmative* requirements, that is, to rules that a cable station *must* carry a certain program or channel or type of program or channel, and does not prohibit negative requirements, that is, rules prohibiting cable stations from carrying certain signals. . . .

. . .

However, having consulted the legislative history, we cannot agree with the Commission's contention that, as used in Section 544(f), the word "requirements" was meant to distinguish between affirmative and negative obligations. Some "negative" rules would probably fall under Section 544(f)'s bar. For instance, a local franchising authority's attempt to *prohibit* the carriage of HBO would likely implicate the same Congressional concerns as an attempt to *require* carriage of HBO. We therefore think Section 544(f) would bar such a prohibition.

On the other hand, not every "affirmative" regulation implicates Section 544(f). Suppose, for instance, a cable company bidding for a local franchise indicated that it was planning to provide service on only Mondays, Tuesdays, and Wednesdays. If the local franchising authority decided that it would award the franchise only to a cable company that agreed to provide service seven days a week, it would not be, in the words of the House report, "dictat[ing] the specific programming to be provided over a cable system" even though the regulation would be affirmative in nature.

In short, we think that the affirmative/negative distinction suggested by the Commission fails to capture what Congress meant by the term "requirements" in Section 544(f). Rather, the examples given in the House report suggest that the key is whether a regulation is content-based or content-neutral. Section 544(f), one must note, does not simply forbid "requirements"; it forbids "requirements regarding the *provision* or *content* of cable services" (emphasis added). The House report suggests that Congress thought a cable company's owners, not government officials, should decide what sorts of programming the company would provide. But it does not suggest a concern with regulations of cable not based on the content of cable programming, and do not require that particular programs or types of programs be provided. Such regulations are not requirements "regarding the provision or content" of cable services.

Syndex is clearly different from a requirement or prohibition of the carriage of a particular program or channel. Although it will certainly affect the content of cable programming, it is content-neutral. . . .

We do not mean to suggest that the concept of content neutrality, as developed in First Amendment cases, can be freely imported into all cases construing the Communications Act. In this case, however, the history reviewed above explicitly shows that Congress's concern in enacting Section 544(f) was with content-based rules. We think it plain that Congress did not intend Section 544(f) to forbid syndex. . . .

. . .

C. The First Amendment

The petitioners argue that syndex rules, like the must-carry rules that this Court struck down in [*Century Communications*], cannot survive even the relaxed First Amendment scrutiny of [*O'Brien*]. However, the Commission was correct to find that the rules are not subject to such scrutiny.

The petitioners repeatedly claim that syndex restrains the expression of fully protected speech which has been paid for and authorized under the compulsory licensing scheme of Section 111 of the Copyright Act. [ ] The fact is, however, that because of the provisions of Section 111, cable companies will *not* be able to obtain a compulsory license to transmit a program if transmission would violate the syndex rules. As explained above, Congress deliberately chose to withhold a compulsory license from those transmissions that the FCC decides to prohibit for reasons of communications policy. The petitioners are therefore in the position of claiming that they have a First Amendment right to express themselves using the copyrighted materials of others.

. . .

In the present case, the petitioners desire to make commercial use of the copyrighted works of others. There is no First Amendment right to do so. Although there is some tension between the Constitution's copyright clause and the First Amendment, the familiar idea/expression dichotomy of copyright law, under which ideas are free but their particular expression can be copyrighted, has always been held to give adequate protection to free expression. [ ]

. . .

IV. Conclusion

"While the deregulation of the cable television industry raises serious policy questions, . . . these questions are best left to the agencies that were created, in large part, to resolve them." [*Malrite*] The Commission has considered anew the question of how to balance the rights of broadcast and cable television companies so as best to serve the public interest in receiving diverse programming. Congress decided that this question should be resolved by the agency, and on the record before us we uphold its resolution.

The petition for review is denied.

Add to casebook p. 431, replacing 1st full paragraph:

The conflict over access channels has another side--produced by the requirement that the cable operator not censor any access material. More than 1,200 of the nation's 8,000 systems offer some form of public access, and an estimated 40,000 hours of public access programming is produced each week. In cities in which access channels exist, they may be opposed by citizens who are offended by what is presented. Some examples from two channels fully devoted to public access in Austin, Texas, are reported in Schwartz, Austin Gets an Eyeful: Sacrilege and the Klan, Channels, Mar./Apr. 1985, at 42-43: (a) in front of a crucifix "a man in a Charles Manson mask dances and chants incoherently about sex and religion;" (b) a Ku Klux Klan leader interviews a man who had been imprisoned for fire-bombing school buses during Detroit's busing controversy; and (c) a Halloween program in which a slimy monster comes out of a nearby lake and kills everything in its path. Some groups wanted to end access, particularly because of the Klan programs.

Apparently, indecency is rarely a problem on the public access channels. "Shows containing nudity are usually more expensive to film and are often shown on other channels, known as leased-access channels, where time is sold for a fee of about $100 a half-hour and commercials are allowed." N.Y. Times, April 13, 1987, at 19. The regulation of indecency is discussed later in this chapter.

Operators of the public access channels are permitted to schedule programs. The Austin channels, for example, extended their hours. One result was that the group that put the Manson program on was moved from 10:30 p.m. to 1 a.m. In San Francisco, the operators scheduled a Klan program for 3:30 p.m. on

Tuesdays and sandwiched it between programs produced by Chinese for Affirmative Action, the Anti-Defamation League, and Jewish Community Relations. San Francisco Chronicle, Dec. 29, 1986, at A6.

Apart from the suits by cable operators seeking to be free of the access requirement, suits are beginning to come from the other direction. In Kansas City, Mo., the Klan failed to get on the access channel. The city had insisted that the franchisee provide an access channel. When the Klan requested access, the operator refused because the show was not locally produced. The Missouri Klan then offered to provide a program featuring interviews with local advocates of white supremacy. The operator agreed to air the show. Before the Klan members could be trained in using the equipment and producing the show, the city council passed legislation converting the channel to a community programming channel under operator control. The operator offered the Klan a guest appearance on a hosted half-hour talk show. The Klan rejected the offer because it had no control over the program. The operator refused to permit the Klan to air its own program.

The ACLU brought suit. One claim was that the city council's action was intended "to suppress the 'racialist' viewpoint" of the Klan. A second argument was that the city, by granting only one cable franchise, has incurred a constitutional obligation to require the operator to provide an access channel. In July 1989, the city council reinstated the access channel, and the case was dropped.

Add to casebook p. 431, after 3rd full paragraph:

One political access provision that is not applicable to cable is the reasonable access requirement of § 312(a)(7). In its 1991 political access NPRM, p. 45 (this supplement), *supra*, the FCC has proposed extending that requirement to cable.

Chapter X

NEW COMMUNICATIONS TECHNOLOGIES

Add to casebook p. 439, after 4th full paragraph:

Initially, there had been some ownership restrictions on MMDS, the most important of which was that a single operator could not acquire a license for more than four of the eight MDS channels in a market. (Remember that an operator could still exceed four channels by leasing other channels from ITFS operators.) The purpose of this restriction was to promote competition between MMDS operators. However, recently, the Commission concluded that competition from other multichannel service providers such as cable was so strong that for even a single MMDS operator to survive in a given market it was necessary that the operator have access to as many channels as possible. Therefore, the Commission voted to eliminate the ownership restrictions. Wireless Cable Service, 68 R.R.2d 429 (1990).

Add to casebook p. 463, after note 1:

1a. The Satellite Home Viewer Act directed the Commission to conduct several inquiries. One of these was to determine "the need for a universal encryption standard that permits decryption of satellite cable programming intended for private viewing." After conducting the required inquiry, the Commission concluded that a mandatory encryption standard would not serve the public interest. The Commission found that there was little need for one because the VC II system had established itself as the *de facto* standard. Furthermore, a mandatory standard would have several negative effects: it would limit technological innovation, increase piracy by restricting technological responses to theft of signals, and it would cause extensive delays in implementing new equipment because of the lengthy standards setting process. Satellite Cable Programming (Universal Encryption Standard), 67 R.R.2d 967 (1990).

1b.   In another inquiry mandated by the Satellite Home
Viewer Act, the FCC found that there was no "pattern
of discrimination by satellite carriers among the
various distributors who market superstation and
network station programming." However, the Commission
did find differences in the rates charged to home dish
distributors and cable operators raising the
possibility that unlawful rate discrimination was
taking place.   After adopting the test for unlawful
discrimination used in proceedings under Section
202(a) of the Communications Act (47 U.S.C.A.
§202(a)), the Commission issued a further notice on
this issue.   "The test in Section 202(a) has three
components: (1) whether the services in question are
like services; (2) whether discrimination has
occurred; and (3) whether such discrimination is just
and reasonable."   Superstation and Network Station
Programming (Discrimination in Distribution), 67
R.R.2d 675 (1990).

Following that inquiry the Commission issued a
report concluding that "there are significant
disparities in some of the prices charged by some
carriers to home dish distributors as compared to the
prices charged to cable companies and other customers
for superstation and network station programming.
Some of these disparities are not justified by the
cost of providing service as documented in this
proceeding." However, the Commission left the final
determination of whether or not these constitute
violations of the Communications Act to hearings on
specific complaints filed by the National Rural
Telecommunications Cooperative. At the same time the
Commission noted that the Satellite Home Viewer Act
provides aggrieved parties a private right of action
in federal court under the Copyright Act.
Superstation and Network Station Programming
(Discrimination in Distribution), 69 R.R.2d 436
(1991).

1c.   Still another provision of the Satellite Home
Viewer Act directed the FCC to extend the syndicated
exclusivity rules to satellite carriers to the extent
it was feasible. After conducting an inquiry into the
matter, the FCC concluded that it was not technically
or economically feasible to subject satellite carriers
to the syndicated exclusivity rules.   Among the
reasons cited for this conclusion were the inability

of the VC II or even the VC II Plus decoders to selectively delete programs in over 200 markets and the much smaller subscriber base (53,900,000 cable subscribers versus 678,000 HSD subscribers) from which to recover the developmental costs of implementing syndicated exclusivity.   Syndicated Exclusivity Requirements for Satellite Carriers, 68 R.R.2d 1172 (1991).

Chapter XI

COPYRIGHT AND TRADEMARK

Add to casebook p. 484, after 2nd full paragraph:

A Supreme Court decision, Feist Publications, Inc. v. Rural Telephone Service Co., Inc., 499 U.S. ____, 111 S.Ct. 1282 (1991), illustrates the principle that facts cannot be copyrighted. Rural Telephone Service, which provides telephone service to several communities in Kansas, publishes a telephone directory. It refused to license its white pages listings to Feist for a larger telephone directory covering 11 telephone service areas. Feist extracted the information from Rural's directory and used it in their own, altering some of the listings and using others identical to the listings in Rural's directory. Rural sued for copyright infringement. The Supreme Court decided in favor of Feist.

Justice O'Connor, writing for the Court, wrote that "[t]his case concerns the interaction of two well-established propositions. The first is that facts are not copyrightable; the other, that compilations of facts generally are. Each of these propositions possesses an impeccable pedigree. . . . [I]t is beyond dispute that compilations of facts are within the subject matter of copyright. Compilations were expressly mentioned in the Copyright Act of 1909, and again in the Copyright Act of 1976. . . . There is undeniable tension between these two propositions. . . . The key to resolving the tension lies in understanding why facts are not copyrightable. The *sine qua non* of copyright is originality. To qualify for copyright protection, a work must be original to the author."

"[T]he copyright in a factual compilation is thin," she wrote. "Notwithstanding a valid copyright, a subsequent compiler remains free to use the facts contained in [another's] publication to aid in preparing a competing work, so long as the competing work does not feature the same selection and arrangement." The Court has rejected, she said, "sweat of the brow" arguments that would give protection to factual compilations on the basis of hard work rather than originality. "Rural expended sufficient effort to make the white pages directory useful," she wrote, "but insufficient creativity to make it original," concluding that the names, towns and telephone numbers copied by Feist were not original to Rural and were therefore not protected by copyright.

Add to casebook p. 485, after 1st full paragraph:

In Community for Creative Non-Violence v. Reid, 490 U.S. 730, 109 S.Ct. 2166 (1989), the Supreme Court was asked to avoid the rigors of section 101(2) by expansively interpreting the term "employee" in section 101(1). It declined. Reid had created a sculpture for CCNV in conformance with CCNV's concept and general design ideas. The parties did not discuss copyright ownership in advance. After the sculpture was finished, each filed a competing copyright claim. The trial judge held that CCNV owned the copyright, but the Court of Appeals for the District of Columbia reversed, holding that it was not a work for hire and therefore the copyright was owned by Reid.

The Supreme Court unanimously affirmed. CCNV did not claim the sculpture was a specially commissioned work under subsection (2); there was no written agreement to that effect, and even if there had been, a sculpture is not one of the types of works to which the subsection applies. Instead, CCNV argued that Reid should be considered an "employee" for purposes of subsection (1), on the ground that CCNV had retained the right to control Reid's product and had actually exercised such control. The Court, however, held that the legislative history of the Act required the term to be understood in light of the general common law of agency, which takes into account many factors in addition to control of the work. It concluded Reid was not an employee because he was engaged in a skilled occupation, supplied his own tools, worked in his own studio, was retained for a brief time for the project in question and no others, had control of his own working hours and the employment and compensation of assistants, and was not treated as an employee for purposes of benefits, social security and payroll taxes, worker's compensation or unemployment taxes.

The Court refused to allow the interpretation given to § 101(1) by the Second Circuit, which had held that freelancers were "employees" if the hiring party had actually wielded control during the creation of the work. See Aldon Accessories Ltd. v. Spiegel, Inc., 738 F.2d 548, cert. denied 469 U.S. 982 (1984). Many publishing and communications companies headquartered in New York apparently had relied on that interpretation and therefore failed to obtain contractual assignments from their freelance contributors. As a result, some industry sources said the *CCNV* decision put in question the ownership of millions of dollars in literary and entertainment properties, and might affect 40 per cent of all existing copyrights.   See Scardino, "The Media Business: A Copyright Ruling Opens a Costly Can of Worms," New York Times, June 12, 1989, at D12.

The decision also generated concern among publishing, communications and entertainment companies because of its effect on termination of copyrights. Licenses and transfers granted by authors generally may be terminated after 35 years by the authors or their survivors; companies that find themselves holding licenses rather than authorship as a result of *CCNV* now have to worry about having their interests terminated altogether.

Magazine publishers often commission freelance photographers or artists to illustrate specific articles. Sometimes they reuse the articles and/or illustrations in books, calendars, special anniversary editions, etc. After the decision in *CCNV*, how may publishers protect their interest in future use of these illustrations?   What is their potential liability for past reuses that may be infringing after *CCNV*?

Add to casebook p. 485, after 4th full paragraph:

It is possible for a copyright owner to sell some rights and retain others. A famous novelist, for example, might first sell the rights to publish excerpts of a forthcoming novel to a national magazine, next sell the right to publish the hardcover first edition of the book to a publishing house, then sell the right for publication of a later paperback edition to another publishing house, and, finally, sell the right to make a movie based on the book to a studio.

It is important to note that the only protections accorded copyright are statutory and are listed in § 106. An unlicensed use that does not conflict with one of the exclusive rights enumerated in § 106 is not an infringement. Beyond that, § 106 is explicitly made subject to a series of limitations listed in §§ 107-118. We will discuss the most important of these limitations, fair use, later in this chapter.

One limitation on the § 106 rights that is not mentioned in the copyright statute is the first sale doctrine. A judicially-created rule, the doctrine provides that copyright owners who sell copies of their copyrighted works have no further control over the sale or lease of those particular copies. The original copyright owners' other rights remain unimpaired.

Under the first sale doctrine, for example, a video store can buy videotapes and then rent them to the public. However, under a 1984 amendment to § 109(b)(1) of the Copyright Act, phonograph records cannot be rented (except by nonprofit libraries or nonprofit educational institutions) without the permission of the copyright holders. The rationale is that there would be little or no purpose in renting a record other than to copy it. In contrast, one can presume that customers may rent videotapes to view them without illegally copying them. For a more complete discussion of the doctrine, see United States v. Atherton, 561 F.2d 747 (9th Cir.1977).

Add to casebook p. 488, after 4th full paragraph:

Two cases illustrate problems of protection of commercial rights to ideas--specifically excluded from copyright coverage under § 102. In one of the cases, Murray v. NBC, 844 F.2d 988, 15 Med.L.Rptr. 1285 (2d Cir.1988), a plaintiff claimed that, four years before "The Cosby Show" premiered on NBC, he had proposed to the network an idea for a half-hour situation comedy starring Cosby to be titled "Father's Day." Unable to sue for copyright infringement, the plaintiff sued for misappropriation, conversion, breach of contract and violation of the Lanham Act (on the theory that the program's origin was falsely designated). The court of appeals held that the plaintiff's idea for a program about an intact, middle-class black family was not novel and could not be protected under copyright under New York law.

In the second case, humorist Art Buchwald announced in 1988 that he was suing Paramount Pictures for $5 million, claiming that the Eddie Murphy movie "Coming to America" was based on a screen treatment Buchwald sold to Paramount in 1983 as a vehicle for Murphy. Buchwald's lawyer said that under the 1983 sale agreement, Buchwald was entitled to a lump sum payment and a share of the net profits from the movie. Like plaintiff Murray, Buchwald sued for breach of contract. Murphy's manager was quoted as saying that so many people were claiming authorship of "Coming to America" that "It's like Zabar's. You [had] better take a number and get in line [to sue]." Mentioning four other suits claiming the idea for the same film, the manager said, "I ought to throw a cocktail party for all these people." New York Times, Nov. 22, 1988 at C19. Buchwald won his breach of contract suit in California Superior Court, Los Angeles County. The court held that evidence demonstrating similarity between Buchwald's screen treatment and "Coming to America," together with evidence of Paramount's unlimited access to Buchwald's idea, warranted a finding that the movie was "based upon" Buchwald's work. Buchwald v. Paramount Pictures Corp., 17 Med.L.Rptr. 1257 (1990). He was awarded damages in the amount of $250,000 plus 19 percent of the profits, but Paramount Pictures denied that there had been any profits.

Buchwald's attorney followed up in May 1990 by filing a Statement of Contentions arguing that Paramount's accounting was bogus and threatening to investigate alleged kickbacks, bribes, drugs and payments to prostitutes raised in other ongoing suits against Paramount. Buchwald's attorney said, "We're dropping the bomb! We found $39.8 million of net profits, minimum." Paramount's attorney labeled the contentions "overblown" and unfounded." The Washington Post, May 17, 1990 at E1.

Add to casebook p. 507, after 2nd full paragraph:

f1. The Second Circuit again addressed the fair use doctrine in New Era Publications International v. Henry Holt & Co., 873 F.2d 576, 16 Med.L.Rptr. 1559 (2d Cir.1989). The case involved a biography by Russell Miller entitled *Bare-Faced Messiah: The True Story of L. Ron Hubbard*. The book contended that Hubbard and the Church of Scientology, which he founded, had glorified Hubbard's image over a period of 30 years through various embellished and distorted accounts of Hubbard's life and activities in Hubbard's own writings and in information put out by the church.

Miller relied in part on information from court records, official documents, interviews and newspaper stories, but in many instances the evidence of alleged discrepancies and distortions came from Hubbard's own unpublished works, such as letters and diaries. Copyright in these works was held by New Era under license from the Church of Scientology, to which Hubbard had bequeathed the rights upon his death.

New Era sought to enjoin publication of the biography in the United States. The case was decided by Judge Leval, who had tried the *Salinger* case. He believed *Bare-Faced Messiah* should be protected as fair use but conceded that "given *Salinger*'s strong presumption against fair use for unpublished materials, I cannot conclude that the Court of Appeals would accord fair use protection to all of Miller's quotations, or that the biography as a whole would be considered non-infringing." he concluded that the book contained 44 passages that would not qualify as fair use under *Salinger*:

Nevertheless, Leval exercised his equitable discretion to deny the injunction. He conceded that injunctive relief is common in copyright cases, but said those typically involve "piracy of artistic creations motivated exclusively by greed." This case was different:

> [A]n injunction would . . . suppress an interesting, well-researched, provocative study of a figure who, claiming both scientific and religious credentials, has wielded enormous influence over millions of people. . . . The abhorrence of the First Amendment to prior restraint is so powerful a force in shaping so many areas of our law, it would be anomalous to presume casually its appropriateness for all cases of copyright infringement. . . .
>
> In the past, efforts to suppress critical biography through the copyright injunction have generally not succeeded because courts (sometimes straining) have found fair use. [ ] The conflict between freedom of speech and the injunctive remedy was thus avoided. Since *Salinger*, however, the issue is inescapable.

He concluded that New Era's damage remedy was adequate to protect its copyright interests with far less harm to First Amendment interests. 695 F.Supp. 1493 (S.D.N.Y.1988).

The Second Circuit affirmed, but only on the ground of laches. (Under the doctrine of laches, if without sufficient justification a plaintiff has delayed bringing an action, and that delay harms the defendant, then the action will be dismissed.) New Era had taken no steps to protect its rights until the book was in print, even though it had known for several years that it was being prepared. "The prejudice suffered by Holt as the result of New Era's unreasonable and inexcusable delay in bringing action invokes the bar of laches." Judge Miner wrote an extended opinion, however, in which the majority rejected Judge Leval's analysis on both the fair use and First Amendment points.

As to fair use, the court said Leval's analysis was too generous to Holt, and as a result the book was a more serious infringement than Leval had concluded. Leval had suggested that use of an author's words to make a point about his character ought to be viewed more favorably than use of an author's words to display the distinctiveness of his writing style. He also urged a distinction between uses to merely "enliven" the text and uses that are necessary to communicate significant points about the subject. The court of appeals rejected both of those suggestions and also disagreed with Leval's conclusion that Miller's book would not affect the market for an authorized biography of Hubbard, which New Era said it planned to commission.

As for Leval's First Amendment concerns, the court was not persuaded "that any first amendment concerns not accommodated by the Copyright Act are implicated in this action. Our observation that the fair use doctrine encompasses all claims of first amendment in the copyright field [ ] has never been repudiated. See, e.g., [*Harper & Row*]. An author's expression of an idea, as distinguished from the idea itself, is not considered subject to the public's 'right to know.' [ ]."

Chief Judge Oakes concurred, but would have affirmed on the merits as well as on the laches ground. He believed there was no proof that *Bare-Faced Messiah* would impair the future market value of Hubbard's writings, that the public interest in encouraging biographical work justified denying the injunction, and that "a non-injunctive remedy provides the best balance between the copyright interests and the First Amendment interests at stake in this case."

Although Henry Holt Co. had prevailed on the laches ground, it took the unusual step of requesting rehearing *en banc* to challenge the panel's conclusions on the fair use issue. The request was denied, 7-5, but it provoked a heated exchange of opinions among the judges of the Second Circuit. 884 F.2d 659, 16 Med.L.Rptr. 2224 (1989).

Chief Judge Oakes (who, as a member of the panel, concurred only on the laches ground) and Judges Newman, Kearse and Winter dissented from the denial of *en banc* consideration. In an opinion by Judge Newman, they said they feared the panel majority opinion would create "misunderstanding on the part of authors and publishers as to the copyright law of this Circuit-- misunderstanding that risks deterring them from entirely lawful writings in the fields of scholarly research, biography, and journalism."

They said denial of the rehearing, "does not mean that this Circuit is committed to the language of the panel opinion . . .." They specifically challenged the portion of the panel opinion refusing to distinguish between copying to enliven text and copying to make a point about the author's character. They also questioned the panel's suggestion that injunctive relief should normally be granted when infringement is threatened. "We do not believe that anything we have said in this opinion concerning fair use or injunctive relief is contrary to the views of a majority of the judges of this court," the dissenters concluded.

Judge Miner, joined by Judges Meskill, Pierce and Altimari (Miner and Altimari were the majority in the panel), wrote a separate opinion to comment on Judge Newman's opinion:

> First, the panel majority opinion is consistent with settled law and leaves no room for misunderstanding. Second, a dissent from a denial of rehearing en banc lacks the authority to dispel misunderstanding in any event. Third, whether or not "this Circuit is committed to the language of the panel opinion," it surely is not committed to the language of the appended dissenting opinion.

On the merits, Judge Miner again rejected the proposed distinction between copying to enliven the copier's prose and copying where necessary to report a fact. He said those considerations were irrelevant once the Court decided--as the panel did in *New Era*--that the purpose-of-use factor favored the copier anyway. "moreover, I question whether judges, rather than literary critics, should decide whether literary material is used to enliven text or demonstrate truth. It is far too easy for one author to use another's work on the pretext that it is copied for the latter purpose rather than the former."

On the appropriateness of injunctive relief, Judge Miner said, "All now agree that injunction is not the automatic consequence of infringement and that equitable considerations always are germane to the determination of whether an injunction is appropriate." He said the statement that "the copying

of 'more than minimal amounts' of unpublished
expressive material calls for an injunction barring
the unauthorized use" with the words, "under ordinary
circumstances."

f2.   A year later the Second Circuit was presented
with another fair use question involving a biography
of L. Ron Hubbard in New Era Publications
International v. Carol Publishing Group, 904 F.2d 152,
17 Med.L.Rptr. 1913 (1990).   An injunction had been
issued against the publication of *A Piece of Blue Sky:
Scientology, Dianetics and L. Ron Hubbard Exposed* by
Jonathan Caven-Atack.   New Era had argued that the
book contained 121 passages drawn from 48 of Hubbard's
published works.   After finding that the copyright on
one of the works quoted had expired, the district
court analyzed the other disputed passages using the
four fair use factors.   According to the district
court, the purpose and character of the use "strongly"
favored New Era because "many of the passages lack any
allowable fair use purpose."   The nature of the
copyrighted work also favored New Era because many of
the quoted passages "are expressive rather than
factual."   The amount used in relation to the
copyrighted work as a whole was still a third factor
favoring New Era because the disputed passages
constituted a "small, but significant element of" the
book.   The court found that the fourth factor, the
effect of the use on the market for the copyrighted
work, did not favor either party.   The court then
issued a permanent injunction listing the 103
infringing passages from 43 published works that had
to be deleted before the biography could be published.
729 F.Supp. 992 (D.C.S.N.Y.1990).

The court of appeals lifted the injunction,
finding that the disputed passages were a fair use.
With regard to the purpose and character of the use,
the court held that critical biographies "fit
'comfortably within' [the] statutory categories 'of
uses illustrative of uses that can be fair.'
[*Salinger*]"   Although the work was intended to be
published for profit, the court distinguished it from
Harper & Row:

However, what the Court [in *Harper & Row*] went
on to consider was the infringer's knowing
exploitation of the copyrighted material--

obtained in an underhanded manner--for an
undeserved economic profit. [ ] The present
case, by contrast, does not involve "an attempt
to rush to the market just ahead of the
copyright holder's imminent publication, as
occurred in *Harper & Row. Salinger* [ ] Instead
. . . the author uses Hubbard's works for the
entirely legitimate purpose of making his point
that Hubbard was a charlatan and the Church a
dangerous cult. To be sure, the author and
appellant want to make a profit in publishing
the book. But the author's use of material "to
enrich" his biography is protected fair use,
"not-withstanding that he and his publisher
anticipate profits." *Id.*

The nature of the copyrighted work also favored
Carol because all of the works quoted were published
works. Further, the court of appeals found that the
works were factual and "the scope of fair use is
greater with respect to factual than non-factual
works."

With regard to the third factor, the amount and
substantiality of the portion used in relation to the
copyrighted work, the court of appeals found that the
quoted passages did not constitute too great a
percentage of the words from which they were taken.
Neither did they "take essentially the heart of
Hubbard's works." Thus, the third factor favored
Carol from both a quantitative and a qualitative
standpoint.

Finally, in analyzing the effect of the biography
on Hubbard's works as well as an authorized biography
that New Era argued it intended to publish, the court
of appeals first noted that:

> even assuming that the book discourages
> potential purchasers of the authorized
> biography, this is not necessarily actionable
> under the copyright laws. Such potential buyers
> might be put off because the book persuaded them
> (as it clearly hopes to) that Hubbard was a
> charlatan, but the copyright laws do not protect
> that sort of injury. Harm to the market for a
> copyrighted work or its derivatives caused by a
> "devastating critique" that "diminished sales by

convincing the public that the original work was of poor quality" is not "within the scope of copyright protection." [ ]

In distinguishing this case from *New Era v. Henry Holt*, the court again focused on the published nature of the works:

> . . . *New Era* involved the publication of previously unpublished material, "particularly from [Hubbard's] early diaries and journals." [ ] Arguably, then, the unfavorable biography in *New Era* threatened economic harm to the authorized biography, even though it fulfilled a different function, because it contained material whose market value 91) had not yet been realized by the copyright holder, and 92) might be entirely misappropriated by the infringing publication. Here, by contrast, the works quoted from all are published, and the book will not tap any sources of economic profit that would otherwise go to the authorized biography.

Having found all four fair use factors to favor Carol, the court of appeals concluded that the book's use of the quoted passages was a fair use and ordered the injunction lifted.

Add to casebook p. 509, after 4th full paragraph:

Unwilling to pass a strong anti-colorizing statute, Congress enacted a compromise version, the National Film Preservation Act of 1988. It allows the Librarian of Congress to select 25 American films each year that are "culturally, historically or esthetically significant" and to require those films to be labeled if they are altered. In such instances a warning label, similar to the one on cigarettes, is placed on video copies of such films: "This is a colorized version of a film originally marketed and distributed to the public in black and white. It has been altered without the participation of the principal director, screenwriter and other creators of the original film."

A related issue is the compression of films-- "lexiconning" or speeding them up imperceptibly to shorten their showing time and thus allow more time for television commercials. Here, too, the creators argue that the film's artistic integrity is violated.

The National Film Preservation Act established the 13-member National Film Preservation Board, representing writers, directors, producers, critics and scholars, to participate in the selection of the 25 films per year. Critic Caryn James, in a 1990 article critical of the law and its ambiguities, said the "coldest, hardest fact of all" is that "a labeling requirement won't stop anyone from coloring or editing a film." She reported that the Board had already met to discuss "the extension of the law, which expires in one year." New York Times, Nov. 8, 1990 at C15.

6. In response to *New Era*, p. 102 (this supplement), *supra*, Rep. Robert W. Kastenmeier (D., Wis.), chairman of the House Judiciary Committee's Subcommittee on Courts, Intellectual Property, and the Administration of Justice, introduced a bill (HR 4263) in March 1990 that would remove any distinction between published and unpublished works for purposes of applying the fair use defense to assertions of copyright infringements. "The chilling effect of the *New Era* decision is obvious and it is real," Kastenmeier said. "The approach to the fair use doctrine" taken by the appeals court "appears to be at odds with Congress' intent in codifying the fair use doctrine in the 1976 Copyright Act." Med.L.Rptr. News Notes, April 3, 1990. At a joint congressional hearing on July 11 about HR 4263 and Senate bill (S 2370), testimony was heard from William F. Patry, policy planning adviser to the U.S. Register of Copyrights and author of a treatise on fair use (taking no position on the legislation but saying Congress should make clear its intent); three Second Circuit judges—Pierre Leval (favoring the legislation as "modest and restrained" and "no more than necessary to eliminate a bias that effectively bars proper historical or journalistic use of unpublished matter"), James L. Oakes (favoring), and Roger J. Miner (opposing the legislation as unnecessary and ineffective); and authors Taylor Branch and J. Anthony Lucas (both commenting on the chilling effect of the Second Circuit decisions). Med.L.Rptr. News Notes, July 24, 1990.

7. U.S. District Court Judge Constance Baker Motley of Manhattan levied a $510,000 fine on Kinko's, the national chain of copying stores, for infringing the copyrights of publishers by photocopying and selling excerpts of books to college students. In Basic Books, Inc. v. Kinko's, a suit brought by eight publishers, Judge Motley said Kinko's had created a new business that "usurped" the copyrights and profits of the publishing industry. She said a large portion of the defendant's earnings have come from selling packets of book excerpts through their 200 stores nationwide. New York Times, Mar. 29, 1991 at D2.

Add to casebook p. 518, after note 4:

5. The National Cable Television Association, Community Antenna Television Association and the Disney Channel filed suit early in 1990 against BMI alleging antitrust violations. The plaintiffs said that the cable industry and its members confront "a cartelized industry in which non-negotiable demands for license fees and terms have been made by the cartel" and are "enforced through punitive copyright infringement litigation." The suit challenges the 50-year practice by BMI of granting, for a price, blanket licenses for public performance of the works of the composers and publishers it represents. In other litigation, American Television & Communications and 16 other cable companies sued BMI and nine affiliates, alleging Sherman Antitrust Act violations. They alleged that BMI and its members are succeeding "in their anticompetitive scheme because of the monopolistic and illegal stranglehold" that they have on the performance rights to music. Broadcasting, Feb. 5, 1990, at 32.

Add to casebook p. 520, at end of 4th paragraph:

Such cases, however, can be difficult to win. For example, although the Boston Athletic Association registered the trademark "Boston Marathon" and licensed one television station to broadcast the race, it was unable to get an injunction prohibiting another station from also televising the event, because it failed to show sufficient evidence of relevant customer confusion.   WCVB-TV v. Boston Athletic Association, 926 F.2d 42, 18 Med.L.Rptr. 1710 (1991).

Chapter XII

DEFAMATION

Add to casebook p. 532, after 1st full paragraph:

In Milkovich v. Lorain Journal Co., the Supreme Court rejected the opinion doctrine.

MILKOVICH v. LORAIN JOURNAL CO.
Supreme Court of the United States, 1990
497 U.S. 1, 110 S.Ct. 2695, 17 Med.L.Rptr. 2009

[Milkovich was coach of the Maple Heights high school wrestling team, which was involved in a brawl with a competing team. The Ohio High School Athletic Association (OHSAA) censured Milkovich and placed his team on probation. Parents of some of the team members sued to enjoin OHSAA from enforcing the probation, contending OHSAA's investigation and hearing violated due process. Milkovich and the school's superintendent, Scott, testified at the hearing on the suit, both denying that Milkovich had incited the brawl through his behavior toward the crowd and a meet official. The judge granted the restraining order sought by the parents. A sports columnist who had attended both the meet and the court hearing wrote about the hearing in a column published the next day in the defendant newspaper. The headline was "Maple beat the law with the 'big lie.'" The theme of the column was that Milkovich and Scott in their testimony at the hearing misrepresented Milkovich's role in the altercation and thereby prevented the team from receiving the punishment it deserved. The concluding paragraphs of the column were as follows:

"Anyone who attended the meet, whether he be from Maple Heights, Mentor [the opposing school] or impartial observer, knows in his heart that Milkovich and Scott lied at the hearing after each having given his solemn oath to tell the truth.

"But they got away with it.

112

"Is that the kind of lesson we want our young people learning from their high school administrators and coaches?

"I think not."

Milkovich and Scott both sued the newspaper, alleging that the column accused them of perjury and thus was libellous per se. After 15 years of litigation and several appeals, the Ohio Court of Appeals held in Milkovich's case that the column was constitutionally protected opinion and granted the newspaper's motion for summary judgment. The Supreme Court reversed.]

CHIEF JUSTICE REHNQUIST delivered the opinion of the Court.

[The opinion reviewed the various constitutional limitations imposed on state libel law in the series of cases beginning with New York Times v. Sullivan. The Court also mentioned its decision in Hustler Magazine, Inc. v. Falwell, p. 571 (the casebook), *infra*, an emotional distress case holding that the First Amendment precluded recovery for an ad parody that "could not reasonably have been interpreted as stating actual facts about the public figure involved."]

. . .

Respondents would have us recognize, in addition to the established safeguards discussed above, still another First Amendment-based protection for defamatory statements which are categorized as "opinion" as opposed to "fact." For this proposition they rely principally on the following dictum from our opinion in *Gertz*:

"Under the First Amendment there is no such thing as a false idea. However pernicious an opinion may seem, we depend for its correction not on the conscience of judges and juries but on the competition of other ideas. But there is no constitutional value in false statements of fact." [ ]

Judge Friendly appropriately observed that this
passage "has become the opening salvo in all arguments
for protection from defamation actions on the ground
of opinion, even though the case did not remotely
concern the question." Cianci v. New Times Publishing
Co. [ ]. Read in context, though, the fair meaning of
the passage is to equate the word "opinion" in the
second sentence with the word "idea" in the first
sentence. Under this view, the language was merely a
reiteration of Justice Holmes' classic "marketplace of
ideas" concept. [ ]

Thus, we do not think this passage from *Gertz* was
intended to create a wholesale defamation exemption
for anything that might be labeled "opinion." Not
only would such an interpretation be contrary to the
tenor and context of the passage, but it would also
ignore the fact that expressions of "opinion" may
often imply an assertion of objective fact.

If a speaker says, "In my opinion John Jones is
a liar," he implies a knowledge of facts which lead to
the conclusion that Jones told an untruth. Even if
the speaker states the facts upon which he bases his
opinion, if those facts are either incorrect or
incomplete, or if his assessment of them is erroneous,
the statement may still imply a false assertion of
fact. Simply couching such statements in terms of
opinion does not dispel these implications; and the
statement, "In my opinion Jones is a liar," can cause
as much damage to reputation as the statement, "Jones
is a liar." As Judge Friendly aptly stated: "[It]
would be destructive of the law of libel if a writer
could escape liability for accusations of [defamatory
conduct] simply by using, explicitly or implicitly,
the words 'I think.'" See *Cianci*, [ ]. It is worthy
of note that at common law, even the privilege of fair
comment did not extend to "a false statement of fact,
whether it was expressly stated or implied from an
expression of opinion." Restatement (Second) of
Torts, supra, § 566 Comment a.

Apart from their reliance on the *Gertz* dictum,
respondents do not really contend that a statement
such as, "In my opinion John Jones is a liar," should
be protected by a separate privilege for "opinion"
under the First Amendment. But they do contend that
in every defamation case the First Amendment mandates

an inquiry into whether a statement is "opinion" or "fact," and that only the latter statements may be actionable.   They propose that a number of factors developed by the lower courts (in what we hold was a mistaken reliance on the Gertz dictum) be considered in deciding which is which.   But we think the "'breathing space'" which "'freedoms of expression require in order to survive,'" [ ], is adequately secured by existing constitutional doctrine without the creation of an artificial dichotomy between "opinion" and fact.

Foremost, we think *Hepps* stands for the proposition that a statement on matters of public concern must be provable as false before there can be liability under state defamation law, at least in situations, like the present where a media defendant is involved.[6]   Thus, unlike the statement, "In my opinion Mayor Jones is a liar," the statement, "In my opinion Mayor Jones shows his abysmal ignorance by accepting the teachings of Marx and Lenin," would not be actionable.   *Hepps* ensures that a statement of opinion relating to matters of public concern which does not contain a provably false factual connotation will receive full constitutional protection.

Next, the *Bresler-Letter Carriers-Falwell* line of cases provide protection for statements that cannot "reasonably [be] interpreted as stating actual facts" about an individual.   [ ]   This provides assurance that public debate will not suffer for lack of "imaginative expression" or the "rhetorical hyperbole" which has traditionally added much to the discourse of our Nation.   [ ]

The *New York Times-Butts* and *Gertz* culpability requirements further ensure that debate on public issues remains "uninhibited, robust, and wide-open." [ ] Thus, where a statement of "opinion" on a matter of public concern reasonably implies false and

---

[6]In *Hepps* the Court reserved judgment on cases involving non-media defendants, [ ], and accordingly we do the same.   Prior to *Hepps* of course, where public-official or public-figure plaintiffs were involved, the *New York Times* rule already required a showing of falsity before liability could result.   [ ]

defamatory facts regarding public figures or officials, those individuals must show that such statements were made with knowledge of their false implications or with reckless disregard of their truth. Similarly, where such a statement involves a private figure on a matter of public concern, a plaintiff must show that the false connotations were made with some level of fault as required by *Gertz*. Finally, the enhanced appellate review required by Bose Corp., provides assurance that the foregoing determinations will be made in a manner so as not to "constitute a forbidden intrusion of the field of free expression." [ ]

We are not persuaded that in addition to these protections, an additional separate constitutional privilege for "opinion" is required to insure the freedom of expression guaranteed by the First Amendment. The dispositive question in the present case then becomes whether or not a reasonable factfinder could conclude that the statements in the . . . column imply an assertion that petitioner Milkovich perjured himself in a judicial proceeding. We think this question must be answered in the affirmative. As the Ohio Supreme Court itself observed, "the clear impact in some nine sentences and a caption is that [*Milkovich*] 'lied at the hearing after . . . having given his solemn oath to tell the truth.'" [ ] This is not the sort of loose, figurative or hyperbolic language which would negate the impression that the writer was seriously maintaining petitioner committed the crime of perjury. Nor does the general tenor of the article negate this impression.

We also think the connotation that petitioner committed perjury is sufficiently factual to be susceptible of being proved true or false. A determination of whether petitioner lied in this instance can be made on a core of objective evidence by comparing, *inter alia*, petitioner's testimony before the OHSAA board with his subsequent testimony before the trial court. As the [Ohio Supreme Court noted in the case of the superintendent] "[w]hether or not H. Don Scott did indeed perjure himself is certainly verifiable by a perjury action with evidence adduced from the transcripts and witnesses present at the hearing. Unlike a subjective assertion the averred defamatory language is an articulation of an objectively verifiable event." 25 Ohio St. 3d, at 252, 496 N.E.2d, at 707. So too with petitioner Milkovich.

The numerous decisions discussed above establishing First Amendment protection for defendants in defamation actions surely demonstrate the Court's recognition of the Amendment's vital guarantee of free and uninhibited discussion of public issues. But there is another side to the equation; we have regularly acknowledged the "important social values which underlie the law of defamation," and recognize that [s]ociety has a pervasive and strong interest in preventing and redressing attacks upon reputation." [*Rosenblatt*]. [ ] Justice Stewart [concurring] in that case put it with his customary clarity:

"The right of a man to the protection of his own reputation from unjustified invasion and wrongful hurt reflects no more than our basic concept of the essential dignity and worth of every human being--a concept at the root of any decent system of ordered liberty.

"The destruction that defamatory falsehood can bring is, to be sure, often beyond the capacity of the law to redeem. Yet, imperfect though it is, an action for damages is the only hope for vindication of redress the law gives to a man whose reputation has been falsely dishonored." [ ]

We believe our decision in the present case holds the balance true. The judgment of the Ohio Court of Appeals is reversed and the case remanded for further proceedings not inconsistent with this opinion.

Reversed.

[Justice Brennan, joined by Justice Marshall, dissented. He said the Court addressed the opinion issue "cogently and almost entirely correctly," and agreed that the lower courts had been under a "misimpression that there is a so-called opinion privilege wholly in addition to the protections we have already found to be guaranteed by the First Amendment . . .." But he disagreed with the application of agreed principles to the facts. ". . . I find that the challenged statements cannot reasonably be interpreted as either stating or implying defamatory facts about petitioner. Under the rule articulated in the majority opinion, therefore, the statements are due 'full constitutional protection.'"

He characterized the columnist's assumption that Milkovich lied as "patently conjecture" and asserted that conjecture is as important to the free flow of ideas and opinions as "imaginative expression" and "rhetorical hyperbole," which the majority agreed are protected. He gave several examples:

> Did NASA officials ignore sound warnings that the Challenger Space Shuttle would explode? Did Cuban-American leaders arrange for John Fitzgerald Kennedy's assassination? Was Kurt Waldheim a Nazi officer? Such questions are matters of public concern long before all the facts are unearthed, if they ever are. Conjecture is a means of fueling a national discourse on such questions and stimulating public pressure for answers from those who know more.

The dissent argued that the language of the column itself made clear to readers that the columnist was engaging in speculation, personal judgment, emotional rhetoric, and moral outrage. "No reasonable reader could understand [the columnist] to be impliedly asserting--as fact--that Milkovich had perjured himself."]

Notes and questions

1. Why does the constitution require protection of rhetorical hyperbole but not opinion? Is rhetorical hyperbole less likely to damage reputation? A more valuable form of speech?

2. The majority says "the statement, 'In my opinion Mayor Jones shows his abysmal ignorance by accepting the teachings of Marx and Lenin,' would not be actionable." If the mayor does not accept the teachings of Marx and Lenin, why is the statement not actionable? Does the Court mean only that the

statement that the mayor is abysmally ignorant is not actionable if the rest of the statement is true?

3.   Would the statements at issue in *Ollman* be actionable under the *Milkovich* principles?

4.   The procedural history of the *Milkovich* case, described at length in omitted portions of the majority opinion, illustrates the persistence and endurance that libel litigation sometimes demands of its participants. The column was published in 1974. Milkovich and Scott filed separate suits.   The Milkovich case went to trial, but the judge directed a verdict for the defendants on the ground that Milkovich was required to show actual malice and had failed to do so. The Ohio Court of Appeals reversed, holding that there was sufficient evidence of actual malice. The Ohio Supreme Court and the Supreme Court of the United States denied review. On remand, the trial court granted defendants' motion for summary judgment on the ground that the column was constitutionally protected as opinion, and alternatively, that Milkovich was a public figure and had failed to make out a *prima facie* case of actual malice. The court of appeals this time affirmed both determinations, but the Ohio Supreme Court reversed, holding that Milkovich was neither a public official nor public figure and that the column was not opinion. The Supreme Court of the United States denied review.

Two years later, Scott's case reached the Ohio Supreme Court. Some judges had been replaced in the interval, and the court now held that the column was constitutionally protected opinion, affirming summary judgment against Scott. Scott v. News-Herald, 25 Ohio St.3d 243, 496 N.E.2d 699 (1986).

The trial court in *Milkovich* granted summary judgment on the opinion ground, and the Ohio Court of Appeals affirmed on the authority of the *Scott* decision. The Ohio Supreme Court denied review, but Milkovich finally won review by the Supreme Court of the United States 16 years after the column appeared.

5. The decision left the Milkovich case unresolved. In a footnote dismissing arguments that independent state grounds precluded Supreme Court review of the opinion issue, the Court recognized that the Ohio

courts still might hold for the defendants on the ground that the state constitution protects opinion or on the ground that Milkovich is a public official or public figure and cannot show actual malice.

6.   Later in 1990, the Supreme Court vacated and remanded a lower court's decision in Immuno AG v. Moor-Jankowski, 74 N.Y.2d 548, 549 N.Y.S.2d 938, 549 N.E.2d 129, 17 Med.L.Rptr. 1161 (1989) for further reconsideration in light of *Milkovich*. Immuno AG, an Austrian pharmaceutical company that performs tests on animals, had sued Moor-Jankowski, editor of the *Journal of Medical Primatology*, published in New York, over a letter to the editor from an animal rights activist concerned about a proposed research facility using chimpanzees for research. When the *Journal* had published the letter, it had included an editor's note saying that Immuno's lawyers had challenged the accuracy of the letter and identifying the writer as an animal rights activist. New York's highest court decided in January 1991 that the state's constitution offers more protection for freedom of the press than does the U.S. Constitution--and dismissed the case. Judge Judith Kaye, writing for the majority, said "We look to our state law because of the nature of the issue in controversy--liberty of the press--where this state has its own exceptional history and rich tradition. 18 Med.L.Rptr. 1625 (1991). The Supreme Court refused June 3, 1991, to review the case for a second time. Med.L.Rptr., News Notes, June 11, 1991.

7. The *Milkovich* distinction between fact and opinion was also an issue in Unelko Corp. v. Rooney, in which the maker of a car windshield treatment product sued Andy Rooney of "60 Minutes" for saying the product "Rain-X" "didn't work." Although Rooney's comment was held to imply an assertion of objective fact and, under *Milkovich*, was not shielded from liability, the U.S. Court of Appeals for the Ninth Circuit upheld a grant of summary judgment for Rooney due to the manufacturer's failure to demonstrate falsity. 912 F.2d 1049, 17 Med.L.Rptr. 2317 (9th Cir.1990).

Add to casebook p. 566, replacing note 14:

14.   A case involving the libel of a judicial candidate in Ohio provided an opportunity for the

Supreme Court to clarify the decision in *Bose* regarding independent appellate review--and simultaneously provided parallels to *Butts*.

HARTE-HANKS COMMUNICATIONS, INC. v. CONNAUGHTON
Supreme Court of the United States, 1989.
109 S.Ct.267, 16 Med.L.Rptr. 1881.

JUSTICE STEVENS delivered the opinion of the Court.

A public figure may not recover damages for a defamatory falsehood without clear and convincing proof that the false "statement was made with 'actual malice'--that is, with knowledge that it was false or with reckless disregard of whether it was false or not." [*New York Times*]. In [*Bose*], we held that judges in such cases have a constitutional duty to "exercise independent judgment and determine whether the record establishes actual malice with convincing clarity." [ ] In this case the Court of Appeals affirmed a libel judgment against a newspaper without attempting to make an independent evaluation of the credibility of conflicting oral testimony concerning the subsidiary facts underlying the jury's finding of actual malice. We granted certiorari to consider whether the Court of Appeals' analysis was consistent with our holding in *Bose*. [ ]

I

Respondent, Daniel Connaughton, was the unsuccessful candidate for the Office of Municipal Judge of Hamilton, Ohio, in an election conducted on November 8, 1983. Petitioner is the publisher of the Journal News, a local newspaper that supported the re-election of the incumbent, James Dolan. A little over a month before the election, the incumbent's Director of Court Services resigned and was arrested on bribery charges. A grand jury investigation of those charges was in progress on November 1, 1983. On that date, the Journal News ran a front page story quoting Alice Thompson, a grand jury witness, as stating that Connaughton had used "dirty tricks" and offered her and her sister jobs and a trip to Florida "in appreciation" for their help in the investigation.

Invoking the federal court's diversity jurisdiction, Connaughton filed an action for damages, alleging that the article was false, that it had damaged his personal and professional reputation, and that it had been published with actual malice. After discovery, petitioner filed a motion for summary judgment relying in part on an argument that even if Thompson's statements were false, the First Amendment protects the accurate and disinterested reporting of serious charges against a public figure. The District Court denied the motion, noting that the evidence raised an issue of fact as to the newspaper's interest in objective reporting and that the "neutral reportage doctrine" did not apply to Thompson's statements. The case accordingly proceeded to trial.

After listening to six days of testimony and three taped interviews--one conducted by Connaughton and two by Journal News reporters--and reviewing the contents of 56 exhibits, the jury was given succinct instructions accurately defining the elements of public figure libel and directed to answer three special verdicts. It unanimously found by a preponderance of the evidence that the November 1 story was defamatory and that it was false. It also found by clear and convincing proof that the story was published with actual malice. After a separate hearing on damages, the jury awarded Connaughton $5,000 in compensatory damages and $195,000 in punitive damages. Thereafter, the District Court denied a motion for judgment notwithstanding the verdict . . ., and petitioner appealed.

The Court of Appeals affirmed. [ ] In a lengthy opinion, the majority detailed why its "independent examination of the entire record" had demonstrated that "the judgment does not pose a forbidden intrusion into the First Amendment rights of free expression" [ ] The opinion identified the "core issue" as "simply one of credibility to be attached to the witnesses appearing on behalf of the respective parties and the reasonableness and probability assigned to their testimony." [ ] It separately considered the evidence supporting each of the jury's special verdicts, concluding that neither the finding that the article was defamatory, nor the finding that it was false was clearly erroneous.

The Court of Appeals' review of the actual malice determination involved four steps. It first noted the wide disparity between the respective parties' versions of the critical evidence, pointing out that if the jury had credited petitioner's evidence it "could have easily concluded that Thompson's charges were true and/or that the *Journal*'s conduct in determining Thompson's credibility was not a highly unreasonable departure from the standards of investigation and reporting ordinarily adhered to by reasonable publishers." [ ] Second, it inferred from the jury's answers to the three special interrogatories that "it obviously elected to assign greater credibility to the plaintiff's witnesses and proof [and that] the jury simply did not believe the defendants' witnesses, its evidentiary presentations or its arguments." [ ] Third, having considered what it regarded as the "subsidiary or operative facts" that comprised the plaintiff's theory of the case, it concluded that the jury's finding concerning those operative facts were not clearly erroneous. [ ] Fourth, "in the exercise of its independent judgment" based on its evaluation of the "cumulative impact of the subsidiary facts," the court concluded "that Connaughton proved, by clear and convincing evidence, that the *Journal* demonstrated its actual malice when it published by the November 1, 1983, article despite the existence of serious doubt which attached to Thompson's veracity and the accuracy of her reports." [ ]

Judge Guy dissented. In his opinion the admissions made by Connaughton in his interview with Journal News reporters the day before the story was published sufficiently corroborated Thompson's charges to preclude a finding of actual malice. [ ] He was satisfied, as a matter of law, that respondent had failed to prove actual malice by clear and convincing evidence, regardless of whether determinations of credibility made by the jury are subject to a *de novo* standard of review. [ ]

II

Petitioner contends that the Court of Appeals made two basic errors. First, while correctly stating the actual malice standard announced in [*New York Times*], the court actually applied a less severe standard that merely required a showing of "'highly unreasonable conduct constituting an extreme departure from the standards of investigation and reporting ordinarily adhered to by responsible publishers.'" [ ] Second, the court failed to make an independent *de novo* review of the entire record and therefore incorrectly relied on subsidiary facts implicitly established by the jury's verdict instead of drawing its own inferences from the evidence.

There is language in the Court of Appeals' opinion that supports petitioner's first contention. For example, the Court of Appeals did expressly state that the Journal News' decision to publish Alice Thompson's allegations constituted an extreme departure from professional standards. Moreover, the opinion attributes considerable weight to the evidence that the Journal News was motivated by its interest in the re-election of the candidate it supported and its economic interest in gaining a competitive advantage over the Cincinnati Enquirer, its bitter rival in the local market. Petitioner is plainly correct in recognizing that a public figure plaintiff must prove more than an extreme departure from professional standards and that a newspaper's motive in publishing a story--whether to promote an opponent's candidacy or to increase its circulation--cannot provide a sufficient basis for finding actual malice.

The language in the Court of Appeals' opinion discussing professional standards is taken from Justice Harlan's plurality opinion in [*Curtis Publishing Co.*]. In that case Justice Harlan had opined that the *New York Times* actual malice standard should be reserved for cases brought by public officials. The *New York Times* decision, in his view, was primarily driven by the repugnance of seditious libel and a concern that public official libel "lay close" to this universally renounced, and long-defunct, doctrine. [ ] In place of the actual malice standard, Justice Harlan suggested that a public figure need only make "a showing of highly unreasonable conduct constituting an extreme departure from the standards of investigation and reporting ordinarily adhered to by responsible publishers." [ ] This proposed standard, however, was emphatically rejected by a majority of the Court in favor of the stricter *New York Times* actual malice rule.   [ ]

Moreover, just four years later, Justice Harlan acquiesced in application of the actual malice standard in public figure cases, [ ], and by the time of the Court's decision in [Gertz], the Court was apparently unanimously of this view. Today, there is no question that public figure libel cases are controlled by the New York Times standard and not by the professional standards rule, which never commanded a majority of this Court.

It is also worth emphasizing that the actual malice standard is not satisfied merely through a showing of ill will or "malice" in the ordinary sense of the term. Indeed, just last Term we unanimously held that a public figure "may not recover for the tort of intentional infliction of emotional distress . . . without showing . . . that the publication contains a false statement of fact which was made . . . with knowledge that the statement was false or with reckless disregard as to whether or not it was true." [Hustler]. Nor can the fact that the defendant published the defamatory material in order to increase its profits suffice to prove actual malice. The allegedly defamatory statements at issue in the New York Times case were themselves published as part of a paid advertisement. [ ] If a profit motive could somehow strip communications of the otherwise available constitutional protection, our cases from New York Times to Hustler Magazine would be little more than empty vessels. Actual malice, instead, requires at a minimum that the statements were made with a reckless disregard for the truth. And although the concept of "reckless disregard" "cannot be fully encompassed in one infallible definition," [ ], we have made clear that the defendant must have made the false publication with a "high degree of awareness of . . . probable falsity," [ ], or must have "entertained serious doubts as to the truth of his publication," [ ].

Certain statements in the Court of Appeals' opinion, when read in isolation, appear to indicate that the court at times substituted the professional standards rule for the actual malice requirement and at other times inferred actual malice from the newspaper's motive in publishing Thompson's story. Nevertheless, when the opinion is read as a whole, it is clear that the conclusion concerning the newspaper's departure from accepted standards and the evidence of motive were merely supportive of the court's ultimate conclusion that the record "demonstrated a reckless disregard as to the truth or falsity of Thompson's allegations and thus provided clear and convincing proof of 'actual malice' as found by the jury." [ ]   Although courts must be careful not to place too much reliance on such factors, a plaintiff is entitled to prove the defendant's state of mind through circumstantial evidence, [ ], and it cannot be said that evidence concerning motive or care never bears any relation to the actual malice inquiry. Thus, we are satisfied that the Court of Appeals judged the case by the correct substantive standard.

The question whether the Court of Appeals gave undue weight to the jury's findings--whether it failed to conduct the kind of independent review mandated by our opinion in *Bose*--requires more careful consideration.   A proper answer to that question must be prefaced by additional comment on some of the important conflicts in the evidence.

II

The most important witness to the bribery charges against the Director of Court Services was Patsy Stephens, Alice Thompson's older sister.   In a tape recorded interview conducted in Connaughton's home between 12:30 and 4:30 a.m. on September 17, 1983, Stephens explained how, on forty or fifty occasions, she had visited with the court administrator, Billy Joe New, in his office and made cash payments to dispose of "DUI" and other minor criminal charges against her former husband and various other relatives and acquaintances.   On September 22, pursuant to an arrangement made by Connaughton at the suggestion of the county prosecutor, Stephens took a lie detector test.   After learning that she had passed the test, Connaughton filed a written complaint against New.   In due course, New was arrested, indicted and convicted.

Alice Thompson was one of the eight persons present at the tape recorded interview on September 17.   One of the cases Patsy Stephens described was a shoplifting charge against her sister.   Thompson volunteered some comments about the incident, but otherwise had little to say during the long interview with Stephens. Thompson was also present on the 22nd, when Stephens took the polygraph test, but Thompson declined to submit to such a test. [ ] On that day, the two sisters spent several hours in the company of Connaughton, his wife, and two of his supporters. They discussed a number of subjects, including the fact that Billy Joe New had just resigned, the question whether there was reason to be concerned about the safety of the two sisters, the fact that Martha Connaughton might open an ice cream parlor sometime in the future, the possibility that the two sisters might be employed there as waitresses, and a vacation in Florida planned by the [Connaughtons] for after the election.

Late in October, New's lawyer, Henry Masana, met with Jim Blount, the editorial director of the Journal News, and Joe Cocozzo, the newspaper's publisher, to arrange a meeting with Alice Thompson. Masana explained that Thompson wanted to be interviewed about the "dirty tricks" Connaughton was using in his campaign. Thereafter, on October 27, Blount and Pam Long, a Journal News reporter, met with Thompson in the lawyer's office and tape-recorded the first of the two statements that provided the basis for the story that Long wrote and the Journal News published on November 1.

The tape of Alice Thompson's interview is one hour and twenty minutes long. Significant portions of it are inaudible or incoherent. It is clear, however, that Thompson made these specific charges:

--that Connaughton had stated his purpose in taping the interview with Patsy Stephens was to get evidence with which he could confront New and Judge Dolan and "scare them into resigning" without making any public use of the tapes;

--that he would pay the expenses for a three week vacation in Florida for the two sisters;

--that he would buy a restaurant for the two sisters' parents to operate;

--that he would provide jobs for both Patsy Stephens and Alice Thompson;

--that he would take them out to a victory dinner at an expensive French restaurant after the election; and

--that Connaughton would not allow knowledge of the sisters' involvement to become public.

During the course of the interview, Thompson indicated that she had told her story to the Cincinnati Enquirer, which declined to print it, [ ], and that the local police, likewise, were not interested, [ ]. Thompson indicated that she was "against" Connaughton becoming a judge. [ ] She also asserted that since Connaughton had made public that she and her sister had provided evidence against New, friends had accused her "of being a snitch and a rat"--epithets to which she took great offense--and that one reason she came to the Journal News was "to get that cleared up." In her description of the interview in Connaughton's home on September 17, Thompson stated that Connaughton had frequently turned off the tape recorder, that his voice would not be heard on the tape, and, somewhat inconsistently (and in response to a leading question), that most of her comments had been made in response to leading questions by Connaughton.

Toward the end of the interview, Blount made two significant comments. He announced that "Pam will, of course, write the story," [ ], and he asked "[w]hat would happen if we called your sister," [ ]. In response to the first comment, Thompson volunteered a somewhat improbable explanation for her motivation in seeking the interview, and in response to second she gave an equivocal answer, even though she had previously assured Blount that Stephens would confirm everything she had said.

On Sunday, October 30, an editorial appeared in the Journal News under the headline "Municipal Court Race will have More than One Loser." [ ] In the column, Blount observed that the campaign "battle has been all it was expected to be and more," and predicted that "[a] lot could still happen in the next eight to nine days." [ ] He went onto discuss the charges pending against New, stating that the "array of charges and counter charges probably has taken some votes from Dolan." [ ] He cautioned, however, that the race was still wide open and quoted an unidentified voter as saying, "I resent voting for a person who I later find has been deceitful or dishonest in campaigning." [ ] Significantly, this unidentified person did not express indignation at dishonesty in the administration of the Municipal Court--a concern one would think the arrest of New might have prompted--but rather, a distaste for dishonesty in *campaigning*--a concern that the then-uninvestigated and unwritten November 1 story would soon engender. After questioning the Cincinnati Enquirer's coverage of a story critical of Dolan and suggesting that "the Connaughton forces have a wealthy, influential link to *Enquirer* decisionmakers," the column indicated that the Journal News had not yet decided which candidate it favored, but implied that an endorsement was forthcoming. [ ]

On October 31st, a reporter for the Journal News telephoned Connaughton and asked him to attend a meeting with Jim Blount, stating "that the endorsement may hang in the balance." [ ] Connaughton met with the reporter, Blount, and Cocozzo that afternoon and discussed a variety of subjects. One of the subjects was the rumor that Connaughton had an influential link to the Cincinnati Enquirer. Connaughton asserted that he had "no extraordinary pull or any inside track to anybody down there," and that any rumor to the contrary was "a lie." [ ] Another subject was Connaughton's participation in the investigation of Billy Joe New. Connaughton provided a chronology of the events that led to his filing of the complaint against New and explained that he believed that he had an obligation "as an attorney and officer of the court to report [New's] crimes." [ ] No mention was made of Thompson's interview or her charges against Connaughton. [ ] After about an hour, Jim Blount received a telephone call and then told Connaughton that a reporter wanted to interview him. [ ]

Connaughton then went into another office where Blount and Long advised him that they had interviewed Alice Thompson and were "trying to find out . . . how much of her statement was true." [ ] The ensuing tape-recorded interview lasted 55 minutes. Connaughton acknowledged that the meetings that Thompson described had taken place and that there had been speculative discussion about each of the subjects

that Thompson mentioned. He stated, however, that
Thompson's account of their meetings was "obviously
shaded   and   bizarre,"   [ ],   and   that   there   was
"absolutely" no "*quid pro quo* for information."

Thus,   while   categorically   denying   that   he
intended to confront New and Judge Dolan with the tape
of   the   Stephens   interview   to   scare   them   into
resigning, Connaughton admitted that he might well
have speculated about what they would say or do if
they heard the tapes. Similarly, while denying that
he had promised Stephens and Thompson anonymity, he
agreed that he had told them that he had hoped that
they could remain anonymous. He also categorically
denied that he had promised Thompson a job as a
waitress, promised Stephens a job at the Municipal
Court, or promised to set their parents up in a
restaurant,   although   he   did   acknowledge   a   general
conversation in which his wife had discussed the
possibility that if her dream of opening "a gourmet
ice cream shop" should materialize, the sisters might
work there.   There were similar acknowledgments of
references   to   a   possible   Florida   trip   and   post-
election victory dinner, but denials of any promises.
At the end of the interview, Long went back--stressing
that Thompson's charge was a "hefty" one--and asked
for a second time whether Connaughton had promised
Stephens a job at the Municipal Court if he was
elected.   He   once   again   unequivocally   denied   the
allegation.

The following day the lead story in the Journal
News--under the headline "Bribery case witness claims
jobs, trip offered--reported that "[a] woman called to
testify before the . . . Grand Jury in the Billy Joe
New bribery case claims Dan Connaughton, candidate for
Hamilton Municipal Judge, offered her and her sister
jobs and a trip to Florida 'in appreciation' for their
help."   [ ]   The article, which carried Pam Long's
byline, stated that Thompson accused Connaughton of
using "'dirty tricks'" to gain her cooperation in
investigating New and that Connaughton, although
admitting that he did meet with Thompson, "denied any
wrongdoing."   [ ]   Each of Thompson's allegations was
accurately   reported,   including   her   claims   that
Connaughton   had   promised   her   "to   protect   her
anonymity," [ ], that he had promised Stephens "a
municipal court job" and Thompson some other sort of

work, that he had invited both sisters on "a post-
election trip to Florida," and that he had offered "to
set up Thompson's parents . . . in the restaurant
business," [ ].   The article conveyed Thompson's
allegations that "the tapes were turned off and on
during a session [that] lasted until 5:30 a.m.," and
that these promises were made "[w]hen the tape was
turned off." [ ] In addition, Long wrote, "Thompson
claimed Connaughton had told her the tapes he made of
her . . . statement . . . were to be presented to
Dolan" with the hope that Dolan might resign, thereby
allowing Connaughton to assume the municipal
judgeship. [ ] Connaughton's contrary version of the
events was also accurately reported.

As the Court of Appeals correctly noted, there
was evidence in the record--both in the Thompson tape
and in the Connaughton tape--that would have supported
the conclusion that Thompson was telling the truth and
that Connaughton was dissembling.   [ ] On the other
hand, notwithstanding the partial confirmation of
Thompson's charges in the Connaughton tape, there
remained a sharp conflict between their respective
versions of the critical events.   There was
unquestionably ample evidence in the record to support
a finding that Thompson's principal charges were
false.   The fact that an impartial jury unanimously
reached that conclusion does not, however, demonstrate
that the Journal News acted with actual malice.
Unlike a newspaper, a jury is often required to decide
which of two plausible stories is correct. Difference
of opinion as to the truth of a matter--even a
difference of twelve to one--does not alone constitute
clear and convincing evidence that the defendant acted
with a knowledge of falsity or with a "high degree of
awareness of . . . probable falsity," [ ]. The jury's
verdict in this case, however, derived additional
support from several critical pieces of information
that strongly support the inference that the Journal
News acted with actual malice in printing Thompson's
false and defamatory statements.

IV

On October 27, after the interview with Alice
Thompson, the managing editor of the Journal News
assembled a group of reporters and instructed them to
interview all of the witnesses to the conversation

between Connaughton and Thompson with one exception--
Patsy Stephens. No one was asked to interview her and
no one made any attempt to do so. [ ] This omission
is hard to explain in light of Blount and Long's
repeated questions during the Connaughton and Thompson
interviews concerning whether Stephens would confirm
Thompson's allegations. [ ] It is utterly
bewildering in light of the fact that the Journal News
committed substantial resources to investigating
Thompson's claims, yet chose not to interview the one
witness who was most likely to confirm Thompson's
account of the events. However, if the Journal News
had serious doubts concerning the truth of Thompson's
remarks, but was committed to running the story, there
was good reason not to interview Stephens--while
denials coming from Connaughton's supporters might be
explained as motivated by a desire to assist
Connaughton, a denial coming from Stephens would
quickly put an end to the story.

The remaining six witnesses, including
Connaughton, were all interviewed separately on
October 31. Each of them denied Alice Thompson's
charges and corroborated Connaughton's version of the
events. Thus, one Journal News reporter testified at
trial that Jeanette and Ernest Barnes denied that any
promises, offers, or inducements were made and that he
had known the Barnes for several years and considered
them both credible. [ ] Another reporter testified
that she interviewed Dave Berry and that Berry stated
that absolutely no promises or offers were made. [ ]
By the time the November 1 story appeared, six
witnesses had consistently and categorically denied
Thompson's allegations, yet the newspaper chose not to
interview the one witness that both Thompson and
Connaughton claimed would verify their conflicting
accounts of the relevant events.

The newspaper's decision not to listen to the
tapes of the Stephens interview in Connaughton's home
also supports the finding of actual malice. During
the Connaughton interview, Long and Blount asked if
they could hear the tapes. [ ] Connaughton agreed,
[ ], and later made the tapes available, [ ]. Much of
what Thompson had said about the interview could
easily have been verified or disproven by listening to
the tapes. Listening to the tapes, for example, would
have revealed whether Thompson accurately reported

that the tape recorders were selectively turned on and off and that Connaughton was careful not to speak while the recorders were running. Similarly, the tapes presented a simple means of determining whether Stephens and Thompson had been asked leading questions, as Thompson claimed. Furthermore, if Blount was truly in equipoise about the question whether to endorse the incumbent for re-election--as he indicated in the column that he published on Sunday, October 30--it is difficult to understand his lack of interest in a detailed description of the corrupt disposition of 40 to 50 cases in Judge Dolan's court. Even though he may have correctly assumed that the account did not reflect on the integrity of the judge himself, surely the question whether administrative shortcomings might be revealed by the tapes would be a matter in which an editor in the process of determining which candidate to endorse would normally have an interest. Although simply one piece of evidence in a much larger picture, one might reasonably infer in light of this broader context that the decision not to listen to the tapes was motivated by a concern that they would raise additional doubts concerning Thompson's veracity.

Moreover, although just a small part of the larger picture, Blount's October 30 editorial can be read to set the stage for the November 1 article. Significantly, this editorial appeared before Connaughton or any of the other witnesses were interviewed. Its prediction that further information concerning the integrity of the candidates might surface in the last few days of the campaign can be taken to indicate that Blount had already decided to publish Thompson's allegations, regardless of how the evidence developed and regardless of whether or not Thompson's story was credited upon ultimate reflection.

Finally, discrepancies in the testimony of Journal News witnesses may have given the jury the impression that the failure to conduct a complete investigation involved a deliberate effort to avoid the truth. Thus, for example, Blount's superiors testified that they understood that Blount had directed reporter Tom Grant to ask the police whether Thompson had repeated her charges against Connaughton to them and whether they considered her a credible witness. [ ] Blount also so testified. [ ] Grant, however, denied that he had been given such an assignment. [ ] Similarly, at the early stages of the proceeding, there was testimony that on October 31 Pam Long had tried to arrange a meeting with Patsy Stephens over the telephone, [ ], that Blount was standing at her desk during the conversation and overheard Long talking to Stephens, [ ], and that Connaughton had volunteered that he would have Stephens get in touch with them, [ ]. Connaughton categorically denied that the issue of getting in touch with Stephens was ever discussed, [ ], and ultimately Blount and Long agreed that there was no contact--and no attempt to make contact--with Stephens on the 31 or at any other time before the story was published, [ ].

V

The question whether the evidence in the record in a defamation case is sufficient to support a finding of actual malice is a question of law. [ ] This rule is not simply premised on common law tradition, but on the unique character of the interest protected by the actual malice standard. Our profound national commitment to the free exchange of ideas, as enshrined in the First Amendment, demands that the law of libel carve out an area of "'breathing space'" so that protected speech is not discouraged. [ ] The meaning of terms such as "actual malice"--and, more particularly, "reckless disregard"--however, are not readily captured in "one infallible definition." [ ] Rather, only through the course of case-by-case adjudication can we give content to these otherwise elusive constitutional standards. [ ] Moreover, such elucidation is particularly important in the area of free speech for precisely the same reason that the actual malice standard is itself necessary. Uncertainty as to the scope of the constitutional protection can only dissuade protected speech--the more elusive the standard, the less protection it affords. Most fundamentally, the rule is premised on the recognition that "[j]udges, as expositors of the Constitution," have a duty to "independently decide whether the evidence in the record is sufficient to cross the constitutional threshold that bars the entry of any judgment that is not supported by clear and convincing proof of 'actual malice.'" [ ]

There is little doubt that "public discussion of the qualifications of a candidate for elective office presents what is probably the strongest possible case for application of the *New York Times* rule," [ ], and the strongest possible case for independent review. As Madison observed in 1800, just nine years after ratification of the First Amendment:

> "Let it be recollected, lastly, that the right of electing the members of the government constitutes more particularly the essence of a free and responsible government. The value and efficacy of this right depends on the knowledge of the comparative merits and demerits of the candidates for public trust, and on the equal freedom, consequently, of examining and discussing these merits and demerits of the candidates respectively." [ ]

This value must be protected with special vigilance. When a candidate enters the political arena, he or she "must expect that the debate will sometimes be rough and personal," [ ], and cannot "'cry Foul!' when an opponent or an industrious reporter attempts to demonstrate" that he or she lacks the "sterling integrity" trumpeted in campaign literature and speeches, [ ]. Vigorous reportage of political campaigns is necessary for the optimal functioning of democratic institutions and central to our history of individual liberty.

We have not gone so far, however, as to accord the press absolute immunity in its coverage of public figures or elections. If a false and defamatory statement is published with knowledge of falsity or a reckless disregard for the truth, the public figure may prevail. [ ] A "reckless disregard" for the truth, however, requires more than a departure from reasonably prudent conduct. "There must be sufficient evidence to permit the conclusion that the defendant in fact entertained serious doubts as to the truth of his publication." [ ] The standard is a subjective one--there must be sufficient evidence to permit the conclusion that the defendant actually had a "high degree of awareness of . . . probable falsity." [ ] As a result, failure to investigate before publishing, even when a reasonably prudent person would have done so, is not sufficient to establish reckless disregard.

[ ] In a case such as this involving the reporting of a third party's allegations, "recklessness may be found where there are obvious reasons to doubt the veracity of the informant or the accuracy of his reports." [ ]

In determining whether the constitutional standard has been satisfied, the reviewing court must consider the factual record in full. Although credibility determinations are reviewed under the clearly erroneous standard because the trier of fact has had the "opportunity to observe the demeanor of the witnesses," [ ] the reviewing court must "'examine for [itself] the statements in issue and the circumstances under which they were made to see . . . whether they are of a character which the principles of the First Amendment . . . protect,'" [ ]. Based on our review of the entire record, we agree with the Court of Appeals that the evidence did in fact support a finding of actual malice. Our approach, however, differs somewhat from that taken by the Court of Appeals.

In considering the actual malice issue, the Court of Appeals identified 11 subsidiary facts that the jury "could have" found. [ ] The court held that such findings would not have been clearly erroneous, [ ], and, based on its independent review, that when considered cumulatively they provide clear and convincing evidence of actual malice, [ ]. We agree that the jury *may* have found each of those facts, but conclude that the case should be decided on a less speculative ground. Given the trial court's instructions, the jury's answers to the three special interrogatories, and an understanding of those facts not in dispute, it is evident that the jury *must* have rejected (1) the testimony of petitioner's witnesses that Stephens was not contacted simply because Connaughton failed to place her in touch with the newspaper; (2) the testimony of Blount that he did not listen to the tapes simply because he thought they would provide him with no new information; and (3) the testimony of those Journal News employees who asserted that they believed Thompson's allegations were substantially true. When these findings are considered alongside the undisputed evidence, the conclusion that the newspaper acted with actual malice inextricably follows.

There is no dispute that Thompson's charges had been denied not only by Connaughton, but also by five other witnesses before the story was published. Thompson's most serious charge--that Connaughton intended to confront the incumbent judge with the tapes to scare him into resigning and otherwise not to disclose the existence of the tapes--was not only highly improbable, but inconsistent with the fact that Connaughton had actually arranged a lie detector test for Stephens and then delivered the tapes to the police. These facts were well-known to the Journal News before the story was published. Moreover, because the newspaper's interviews of Thompson and Connaughton were captured on tape, there can be no dispute as to what was communicated, nor how it was said. The hesitant, inaudible and sometimes unresponsive and improbable tone of Thompson's answers to various leading questions raise obvious doubts about her veracity. Moreover, contrary to petitioner's contention that the prepublication interview with Connaughton confirmed the factual basis of Thompson's statements, [ ], review of the tapes makes clear that Connaughton unambiguously denied each allegation of wrongful conduct. Connaughton's acknowledgment, for instance, that his wife may have discussed with Stephens and Thompson the possibility of working at an ice cream store that she might someday open, hardly confirms the allegations that Connaughton had promised to buy a restaurant for the [sisters'] parents to operate, that he would provide Stephens with a job at the municipal court, or even that he would provide Thompson with suitable work. It is extraordinarily unlikely that the reporters missed Connaughton's denials simply because he confirmed certain aspects of Thompson's story.

It is also undisputed that Connaughton made the tapes of the Stephens interview available to the Journal News and that no one at the newspaper took the time to listen to them. Similarly, there is no question that the Journal News was aware that Patsy Stephens was a key witness and that they failed to make any effort to interview her. Accepting the jury's determination that petitioner's explanations for these omissions were not credible, it is likely that the newspaper's inaction was a product of a deliberate decision not to acquire knowledge of facts that might confirm the probable falsity of Thompson's

charges.   Although failure to investigate will not
alone support a finding of actual malice, [ ], the
purposeful avoidance of the truth is in a different
category.

There is a remarkable similarity between this
case--and in particular, the newspaper's failure to
interview Stephens and failure to listen to the tape
recording of the September 17 interview at
Connaughton's home--and the facts that supported the
Court's judgment in [*Curtis Publishing Co.*].   In
[*Curtis Publishing Co.*] the evidence showed that the
Saturday Evening Post had published an accurate
account of an unreliable informant's false description
of the Georgia athletic director's purported agreement
to "fix" a college football game.   Although there was
reason to question the informant's veracity, just as
there was reason to doubt Thompson's story, the
editors did not interview a witness who had the same
access to the facts as the informant and did not look
at films that revealed what actually happened at the
game in question.   This evidence of an intent to avoid
the truth was not only sufficient to convince the
plurality that there had been an extreme departure
from professional publishing standards, but it was
also sufficient to satisfy the more demanding *New York
Times* standard applied by Chief Justice Warren,
Justice Brennan and Justice White.

As in [*Curtis Publishing Co.*], the evidence in
the record of this case, when reviewed in its
entirety, is "unmistakably" sufficient to support a
finding of actual malice.   The judgment of the Court
of Appeals is accordingly

Affirmed.

JUSTICE WHITE, with whom THE CHIEF JUSTICE joins,
concurring.

In my view, in cases like this the historical
facts--e.*g.*, who did what to whom and when--are
reviewable only under the clearly erroneous standard
mandated by Rule 52.   Credibility determinations fall
in this category as does the issue of knowledge of
falsity.   But as I observed in dissent in [*Bose*], the
reckless disregard component of the *New York Times v.
Sullivan* "actual malice" standard is not a question of

historical fact. A trial court's determination of
that issue therefore is to be reviewed independently
by the appellate court.

As I read it, the Court's opinion is consistent
with these views, and--as Justice Kennedy observes--is
consistent with the views expressed by Justice Scalia
in his concurrence. Based on these premises, I join
the Court's opinion.

JUSTICE BLACKMUN, concurring.

I agree with the majority's analysis and with the
result it reaches. I write separately, however to
stress two points.

First . . . [p]etitioner has abandoned the
defense of truth, [ ], despite the fact that there
might be some support for that defense. . . . In
addition, petitioner has eschewed any reliance on the
"neutral reportage" defense. [ ] This strategic
decision appears to have been unwise in light of the
facts of this case. . . .

Second, I wish to emphasize that the form and
content of the story are relevant not only to the
falsity and neutral reportage questions, but also to
the question of actual malice. . . . Under our
precedents, I find significant the fact that the
article in this case accurately portrayed Thompson's
allegations *as* allegations, and also printed
Connaughton's partial denial of their truth. The form
of the story in this case is markedly different from
the form of the story in [*Butts*], where the
informant's description of the events was presented as
truth rather than as contested allegations. . . .

          . . .

I am confident, however, that . . . the
majority's opinion cannot fairly be read to hold that
the content of the article is irrelevant to the actual
malice inquiry. Because I am convinced that the
majority has considered the article's content and form
in the course of its painstaking "review of the entire
record," [ ], and because I conclude that the result
the majority reaches is proper even when the contents
of the story are given due weight, I concur.

JUSTICE KENNEDY, concurring.

I join the opinion of the Court, for in my view it is not inconsistent with the analysis set out in Justice Scalia's separate concurrence.

JUSTICE SCALIA, concurring in the judgment.

I agree with the Court's disposition of this case, and with its resolution of the second legal issue on which we granted certiorari, namely whether "highly unreasonable conduct constituting an extreme departure from ordinary standards of investigation and reporting" is alone enough to establish (rather than merely evidence of) the malice necessary to assess liability in public-figure libel cases.

I disagree, however, with the Court's approach to resolving the first and most significant question upon which certiorari was granted, which was the following:

> "Whether, in a defamation action instituted by a candidate for public office, the First and Fourteenth Amendments obligate an appellate court to conduct an independent review of the entire factual basis for a jury's finding of actual malice--a review that examines both the subsidiary facts underlying the jury's finding of actual malice and the jury's ultimate finding of actual malice itself."

That question squarely raised the conflict that the Sixth Circuit perceived it had created with an earlier decision of the District of Columbia Circuit, en banc, concerning the requirements we set forth in [Bose], that judges "exercise independent judgment" on the question "whether the record establishes actual malice with convincing clarity," [ ].   The nub of the conflict, which is of overwhelming importance in libel actions [by] public figures, is whether this means . . . that the trial judge and reviewing courts must make their own "independent" assessment of the facts allegedly establishing malice; or rather, . . . that they must merely make their own "independent" assessment that, *assuming all of the facts that could reasonably be found in favor of the plaintiff were found in favor of the plaintiff*, clear and convincing proof of malice was established.

Today's opinion resolves this issue in what seems to me a peculiar manner. The Court finds it sufficient to decide the present case to accept, not all the favorable facts that the jury *could reasonably* have found, but rather only the adequately supported favorable facts that the jury *did* find. Exercising its independent judgment just on the basis of those facts (and the uncontroverted evidence) it concludes that malice was clearly and convincingly proved. . . .

While I entirely agree with [the] central portion of the Court's analysis, I do not understand the Court's approach in conducting that analysis only on the basis of the three factual determinations the Court selects. . . .

. . .

In sum, while the Court's opinion is correct insofar as the critical point of deference to jury findings is concerned, I see no basis for consulting only a limited number of the permissible findings. I would have adopted the Sixth Circuit's analysis in its entirety, making our independent assessment of whether malice was clearly and convincingly proved on the assumption that the jury made all the supportive findings it reasonably could have made. This is what common-law courts have always done, and there is ultimately no alternative to it.

Add to casebook p. 571, at end of note 20:

Subsequent court rulings in *Newton* reduced the damages, and a Federal appeals court overturned the award entirely in August 1990. Newton had charged that three NBC news broadcasts in 1980-81 falsely linked him to organized crime figures. A three-judge panel of the United States Court of Appeals for the Ninth Circuit found there was insufficient evidence to show that NBC had either prior knowledge of falsity or reckless disregard of the truth. Newton v. National Broadcasting Co., 18 Med.L.Rptr. 1001 (1990).

Add to casebook p. 578, at end of note 1:

In April 1990 a Connecticut trial court refused to dismiss claims against a radio station alleged to have defamed a woman and to have intentionally inflicted emotional distress by naming her "dog of the week" in the station's weekly "Berate the Brides" segment. Following publication of the woman's picture in a newspaper weddings section, the station's disc jockey is alleged to have said she was "too ugly to even rate" and said she had won a case of Ken-L-Ration and a dog collar. Murray v. Schlosser, 41 Conn.Supp. 362, 17 Med.L.Rptr. 2069 (1990).

Add to casebook p. 580, after 4th full paragraph:

A 1991 case presented the Supreme Court with the question of whether a journalist's use of quotation remarks around words that are not provably the plaintiff's should be treated as reckless disregard for the truth under the actual malice standard.

MASSON v. NEW YORKER MAGAZINE, INC.
Supreme Court of the United States, 1991.
501 U.S. ____, 111 S.Ct. 2419, ___ L.Ed. 2d ____,
18 Med.L.Rptr. 2241.

JUSTICE KENNEDY delivered the opinion of the Court.

In this libel case, a public figure claims he was defamed by an author who, with full knowledge of the inaccuracy, used quotation marks to attribute to him comments he had not made. The First Amendment protects authors and journalists who write about public figures by requiring a plaintiff to prove that the defamatory statements were made with what we have called "actual malice," a term of art denoting deliberate or reckless falsification. We consider in this opinion whether the attributed quotations had the degree of falsity required to prove this state of mind, so that the public figure can defeat a motion for summary judgment and proceed to a trial on the merits of the defamation claim.

I

Petitioner Jeffrey Masson trained at Harvard University as a Sanskrit scholar, and in 1970 became a professor of Sanskrit & Indian Studies at the University of Toronto. He spent eight years in psychoanalytic training, and qualified as an analyst in 1978. Through his professional activities, he came to know Dr. Kurt Eissler, head of the Sigmund Freud Archives, and Dr. Anna Freud, daughter of Sigmund Freud and a major psychoanalyst in her own right. The Sigmund Freud Archives, located at Maresfield Gardens outside of London, serves as a repository for materials about Freud, including his own writings, letters, and personal library.

In 1980, Eissler and Anna Freud hired petitioner as Projects Director of the Archives. After assuming his post, petitioner became disillusioned with Freudian psychology. In a 1981 lecture before the Western New England Psychoanalytical Society in New Haven, Connecticut, he advanced his theories of Freud. Soon after, the Board of the Archives terminated petitioner as Projects Director.

Respondent Janet Malcolm is an author and a contributor to respondent The New Yorker, a weekly magazine. She contacted petitioner in 1982 regarding the possibility of an article on his relationship with the Archives. He agreed, and the two met in person and spoke by telephone in a series of interviews. Based on the interviews and other sources, Malcolm wrote a lengthy article. One of Malcolm's narrative devices consists of enclosing lengthy passages in quotation marks, reporting statements of Masson, Eissler, and her other subjects.

During the editorial process, Nancy Franklin, a member of the fact-checking department at The New Yorker, called petitioner to confirm some of the facts underlying the article. According to petitioner, he expressed alarm at the number of errors in the few passages Franklin discussed with him. Petitioner contends that he asked permission to review those portions of the article which attributed quotations or information to him, but was brushed off with a never-fulfilled promise to "get back to [him]."   [ ]

Franklin disputes petitioner's version of their
conversation. [ ]

The New Yorker published Malcolm's piece in
December 1983, as a two-part series. In 1984, with
knowledge of at least petitioner's general allegation
that the article contained defamatory material,
respondent Alfred A. Knopf, Inc., published the entire
work as a book, entitled In the Freud Archives.

Malcolm's work received complimentary reviews.
But this gave little joy to Masson, for the book
portrays him in a most unflattering light. According
to one reviewer,

"Masson the promising psychoanalytic scholar
emerges gradually, as a grandiose egotist--mean-
spirited, self-serving, full of braggadocio,
impossibly arrogant, and in the end, a self
destructive fool. But it is not Janet Malcolm
who calls him such: his own words reveal this
psychological profile--a self-portrait offered
to us through the efforts of an observer and
listener who is, surely, as wise as any in the
psychoanalytic profession." Coles, Freudianism
Confronts Its Malcontents, Boston Globe, May
27,1984, pp. 58, 60.

Petitioner wrote a letter to the New York Times
Book Review calling the book "distorted."   In
response, Malcolm stated:

"Many of [the] things Mr. Masson told me (on
tape) were discreditable to him, and I felt it
best not to include them. Everything I do quote
Mr. Masson as saying was said by him, almost
word for word. (The 'almost' refers to changes
made for the sake of correct syntax.) I would
be glad to play the tapes of my conversation
with Mr. Masson to the editors of The Book
Review whenever they have 40 or 50 short hours
to spare.) [ ]

Petitioner brought an action for libel under
California law in the United States District Court for
the Northern District of California. During extensive
discovery and repeated amendments to the complaint,
petitioner concentrated on various passages alleged to

be defamatory, dropping some and adding others. The tape recordings of the interviews demonstrated that petitioner had, in fact, made statements substantially identical to a number of the passages, and those passages are no longer in the case. We discuss only the passages relied on by petitioner in his briefs to this Court.

Each passage before us purports to quote a statement made by petitioner during the interviews. Yet in each instance no identical statement appears in the more than 40 hours of taped interviews. Petitioner complains that Malcolm fabricated all but one passage; with respect to that passage, he claims Malcolm omitted a crucial portion, rendering the remainder misleading.

(a) *"Intellectual Gigolo."* Malcolm quoted a description by petitioner of his relationship with Eissler and Anna Freud as follows: "'Then I met a rather attractive older graduate student and I had an affair with her. One day, she took me to some art event, and she was sorry afterward. She said, "Well, it is very nice sleeping with you in your room, but you're the kind of person who should never leave the room--you're just a social embarrassment anywhere else, though you do fine in your own room." And you know, in their way, if not in so many words, Eissler and Anna Freud told me the same thing. They like me well enough "in my own room." They loved to hear from me what creeps and dolts analysts are. I was like an intellectual gigolo--you get your pleasure from him, but you don't take him out in public. . . .'" [ ]

The tape recordings contain the substance of petitioner's reference to his graduate student friend, [ ], but no suggestion that Eissler or Anna Freud considered him, or that he considered himself, an "intellectual gigolo.'" Instead, petitioner said:

"They felt, in a sense, I was a private asset but a public liability . . .. They liked me when I was alone in their living room, and I could talk and chat and tell them the truth about things and they would tell me. But that I was, in a sense, much too junior within the hierarchy of analysis for these important

training analysts to be caught dead with me."
[ ]

(b)   *"Sex, Women, Fun."*   Malcolm quoted
petitioner as describing his plans for Maresfield
Gardens, which he had to occupy after Anna Freud's
death:

> "'It was a beautiful house, but it was dark and
> somber and dead. Nothing ever went on there. I
> was the only person who ever came. I would have
> renovated it, opened it up, brought it to life.
> Maresfield Gardens would have been a center of
> scholarship, but it would also have been a place
> of sex, women, fun. It would have been like the
> change in *The Wizard of Oz*, from black-and-white
> into color.'" [ ]

The tape recordings contain a similar statement, but
in place of the reference to "sex, women, fun," and
The Wizard of Oz, petitioner commented;

> "[I]t is an incredible storehouse. I mean, the
> library, Freud's library alone is priceless in
> terms of what it contains: all his books with
> his annotations in them; the Schreber case
> annotated, that kind of thing.   It's
> fascinating." [ ]

Petitioner did talk, earlier in the interview, of his
meeting with a London analyst:

> "I like him. So, and we got on very well. That
> was the first time we ever met and you know, it
> was buddy-buddy, and we were to stay with each
> other and [laughs] we were going to have a great
> time together when I lived in the Freud house.
> We'd have great parties there and we were
> [laughs]-- . . .   ". . . going to really,
> we were going to live it up." [ ]

(c)   *"It Sounded Better."* Petitioner spoke with
Malcolm about the history of his family, including the
reasons his grandfather changed the family from
Moussaieff to Masson, and why petitioner adopted the
abandoned family name as his middle name. The article
contains the passage:

"'My father is a gem merchant who doesn't like to stay in any one place too long. His father was a gem merchant, too--a Bessarabian gem merchant, named Moussaieff, who went to Paris in the twenties and adopted the name Masson. My parents named me Jeffrey Lloyd Masson, but in 1975 I decided to change my middle name to Moussaieff--it sounded better.'" [ ]

In the most similar tape recorded statement, Masson explained at considerable length that his grandfather had changed the family name from Moussaieff to Masson when living in France, "[j]ust to hide his Jewishness." Petitioner had changed his last name back to Moussaieff, but his then wife Terry objected that "nobody could pronounce it and nobody knew how to spell it, and it wasn't the name that she knew me by." Petitioner had changed his name to Moussaieff because he "just liked it." "[I]t was sort of part of analysis: a return to the roots, and your family tradition and so on." In the end, he had agreed with Terry that "it wasn't her name after all," and used Moussaieff as a middle instead of a last name. [ ]

(d) *"I Don't Know Why I Put It In."* The article recounts part of conversation between Malcolm and petitioner about the paper petitioner presented at his 1981 New Haven lecture:

"[I] asked him what had happened between the time of the lecture and the present to change him from a Freudian psychoanalyst with somewhat outre views into the bitter and belligerent anti-Freudian he had become.

"Masson sidestepped my question. 'You're right, there was nothing disrespectful of analysis in that paper,' he said. 'That remark about the sterility of psychoanalysis was something I tacked on at the last minute, and it was totally gratuitous. I don't know why I put it in.'" [ ]

The tape recordings instead contain the following discussion of the New Haven lecture:

Masson: "So they really couldn't judge the material. And, in fact, until the last sentence

I they were quite fascinated. I think the last
sentence was an in, [sic] possibly, gratuitously
offensive way to end a paper to a group of
analysts.   Uh,--"

Malcolm: "What were the circumstances under
which you put it [in]?. . ."

Masson: "That it was, was true.

          . . .

          ". . .   I really believe it.   I didn't
believe anybody would agree with me.

          . . .

          ". . .   But I felt I should say something
because the papers still sell within the
analytic tradition in a sense. . . .

          . . .

          ". . . It's really not a deep criticism of
Freud.   It contains all the material that would
allow one to criticize Freud but I didn't really
do it.   And then I thought, I really must say
one thing that I really believe, that's not
going to appeal to anybody and that was the very
last sentence.   Because I really do believe
psychoanalysis is entirely sterile. . . ." [ ]

     (e)   *"Greatest Analyst Who Ever Lived."*   The
article contains the following self-explanatory
passage:

     "A few days after my return to New York,
Masson, in a state of elation, telephoned me to
say that Farrar, Straus & Giroux has taken The
Assault on Truth [Masson's book]. 'Wait till it
reaches the best seller list, and watch how the
analysts will crawl,' he crowed.   'They move
whichever way the wind blows. They will want me
back, they will say that Masson is a great
scholar, a major analyst--after Freud, he's the
greatest analyst who ever lived.   Suddenly
they'll be calling, begging, cajoling: "Please
take back what you've said about our profession;

our patients are quitting." They'll try a short smear campaign, then they'll try to buy me, and ultimately they'll have to shut up. Judgment will be passed by history. There is no possible refutation of this book. It's going to cause a revolution in psychoanalysis. Analysis stands or falls with me now.'" [ ]

This material does not appear in the tape recordings. Petitioner did make the following statements on related topics in one of the taped interviews with Malcolm:

> ". . . I assure you when that book comes out, which I honestly believe is an honest book, there is nothing, you know, mean-minded about it. It's the honest fruit of research and intellectual toil. And there is not an analyst in the country who will say a single word in favor of it." [ ]

> "Talk to enough analysts and get them right down to these concrete issues and you watch how different it is from my position. It's utterly the opposite and that's finally what I realized, that I hold a position that no other analyst holds, including, alas, Freud. At first I thought: Okay, it's me and Freud against the rest of the analytic world, or me and Freud and Anna Freud and Kur[t] Eissler and Vic Calef and Brian Bird and Sam Lipton against the rest of the world. Not so, it's me. It's me alone." [ ]

The tape of this interview also contains the following exchange between petitioner and Malcolm:

Masson: ". . . analysis stands or falls with me now."

Malcolm: "Well that's a very grandiose thing to say."

Masson: "Yeah, but it's got nothing to do with me. It's got to do with the things I discovered." [ ]

(f) *"He Had The Wrong Man."* In discussing the
Archives' board meeting at which petitioner's
employment was terminated, Malcolm quotes petitioner
as giving the following explanations of Eissler's
attempt to extract a promise of confidentiality:

> "'[Eissler] was always putting moral pressure on
> me. "Do you want to poison Anna Freud's last
> days? Have you no heart? You're going to kill
> the poor old woman." I said to him, "What have
> I done? *You're* doing it. *You're* firing me.
> What am I supposed to do--be grateful to you?"
> "You could be silent about it. You could
> swallow it. I know it is painful for you. But
> you could just live with it in silence." "Why
> should I do that?" "Because it is the honorable
> thing to do."   Well, he had the wrong man.'"
> [ ]

From the tape recordings, on the other hand, it
appears that Malcolm deleted part of petitioner's
explanation (italicized below), and petitioner argues
that the "wrong man" sentence relates to something
quite different from Eissler's entreaty that silence
was "the honorable thing." In the tape recording,
petitioner states:

> "But it was wrong of Eissler to do that,
> you know. He was constantly putting various
> kinds of moral pressure on me and, 'Do you want
> to poison Anna Freud's last days? Have you no
> heart?'   He called me: 'Have you no heart?
> You're going to kill the poor old woman. Have
> you no heart? Think of what she's done for you
> and you are now willing to do this to her.' I
> said, 'What have I, what have I done? *You* did
> it. You fired me. What am I supposed to do:
> thank you? be grateful to you?' He said, 'Well
> you could never talk about it. You could be
> silent about it. You could swallow it. I know
> it's painful for you but just live with it in
> silence.' 'Fuck you,' I said, 'Why should I do
> that? Why? You know, why should one do that?'
> 'Because it's the honorable thing to do *and you
> will save face. And who knows? If you never
> speak about it and you quietly and humbly accept
> our judgment, who knows that in a few years if*

we don't bring you back?'   Well, he had the
wrong man." App. 215-215.

Malcolm submitted to the District Court that not
all of her discussions with petitioner were recorded
on tape, in particular conversations that occurred
while the two of them walked together or traveled by
car, while petitioner stayed at Malcolm's home in New
York, or while her tape recorder was inoperable. She
claimed to have taken notes of these unrecorded
sessions, which she later typed, then discarding the
handwritten originals. Petitioner denied that any
discussion relating to the substance of the article
occurred during his stay at Malcolm's home in New
York, that Malcolm took notes during any of their
conversations, or that Malcolm gave any indication
that her tape recorder was broken.

Respondents moved for summary judgment. The
parties agreed that petitioner was a public figure and
so could escape summary judgment only if the evidence
in the record would permit a reasonable finder of
fact, by clear and convincing evidence, to conclude
that respondents published a defamatory statement with
actual malice as defined by our cases. [*Liberty
Lobby*] The District Court analyzed each of the
passages and held that the alleged inaccuracies did
not raise a jury question. The court found that the
allegedly fabricated quotations were either
substantially true, or were "'one of a number of
possible rational interpretations' of a conversation
or event that 'bristled with ambiguities,'" and thus
were entitled to constitutional protection, 686 F.
Supp. 1396, 1399 (1987) (quoting [*Bose*]). The court
also ruled that the "he had the wrong man" passage
involved an exercise of editorial judgment upon which
the courts could not intrude. [ ]

The Court of Appeals affirmed, with one judge
dissenting. 895 F.2d 1535 (CA9 1989). The court
assumed for much of its opinion that Malcolm had
deliberately altered each quotation not found on the
tape recordings, but nevertheless held that petitioner
failed to raise a jury question of actual malice, in
large part for the reasons stated by the District
Court. In its examination of the "intellectual
gigolo" passage, the court agreed with the District
Court that petitioner could not demonstrate actual

malice because Malcolm had not altered the substantive content of petitioner's self-description, but went on to note that it did not consider the "intellectual gigolo" passage defamatory, as the quotation merely reported Kurt Eissler's and Anna Freud's opinions about petitioner. In any event, concluded the court, the statement would not be actionable under the "'incremental harm branch' of the 'libelproof' doctrine," id., at 1541 (quoting [Herbert]).

The dissent argued that any intentional or reckless alternation would prove actual malice, so long as a passage within quotation marks purports to be a verbatim rendition of what was said, contains material inaccuracies, and is defamatory 895 F.2d, at 1562-1570. We granted certiorari, 498 U. S. ___ (1990), and now reverse.

II

A

Under California law, "[l]ibel is a false and unprivileged publication by writing...which exposes any person to hatred, contempt, ridicule, or obloquy, or which causes him to be shunned or avoided, or which has a tendency to injure him in his occupation." Cal. Civ. Code Ann. § 45 (West 1982). False attribution of statements to a person may constitute libel, if the falsity exposes that person to an injury comprehended by the statute. [ ] It matters not under California law that petitioner alleges only part of the work at issue to be false. "[T]he test of libel is not quantitative; a single sentence may be the basis for an action in libel even though buried in a much longer text," though the California courts recognize that "[w]hile a drop of poison may be lethal, weaker poisons are sometimes diluted to the point of impotency." [ ]

The First Amendment limits California's libel law in various respects. When, as here, the plaintiff is a public figure he cannot recover unless he proves by clear and convincing evidence that the defendant published the defamatory statement with actual malice, i. e. , with "knowledge that it was false or with reckless disregard of whether it was false or not." [New York Times]. Mere negligence does not suffice.

Rather the plaintiff must demonstrate that the author "in fact entertained serious doubts as to the truth of his publication," [*St. Amant*], or acted with a "high degree of awareness of . . . probable falsity," [*Garrison*].

Actual malice under the *New York Times* standard should not be confused with the concept of malice as an evil intent or a motive arising from spite or ill will. See [*Greenbelt*]. We have used the term actual malice as a shorthand to describe the First Amendment protections for speech injurious to reputation and we continue to do so here. But the term can confuse as well as enlighten. In this respect, the phrase may be an unfortunate one. See [*Connaughton*]. In place of the term actual malice, it is better practice that jury instructions refer to publication of a statement with knowledge of falsity or reckless disregard as to truth or falsity. The definitional principle must be remembered in the case before us.

B

In general, quotation marks around a passage indicate to the reader that the passage reproduces the speaker's words verbatim. They inform the reader that he or she is reading the statement of the speaker, not a paraphrase or other indirect interpretation by an author. By providing this information, quotations add authority to the statement and credibility to the author's work. Quotations allow the reader to form his or her own conclusions, and to assess the conclusions of the author, instead of relying entirely upon the author's characterization of her subject.

A fabricated quotation may injure reputation in at lease two senses, either giving rise to a conceivable claim of defamation. First, the quotation might injure because it attributes an untrue factual assertion to the speaker. An example would be a fabricated quotation of a public official admitting he had been convicted of a serious crime when in fact he had not.

Second, regardless of the truth or falsity of the factual matters asserted within the quoted statement, the attribution may result in injury to reputation because the manner of expression or even the fact that the statement was made indicates a negative personal trait or an attitude the speaker does not hold. John Lennon once was quoted as saying of the Beatles, "We're more popular than Jesus Christ now."   [ ] Supposing the quotation had been a fabrication, it appears California law could permit recovery for defamation because, even without regard to the truth of the underlying assertion, false attribution of the statement could have injured his reputation. Here, in like manner, one need not determine whether petitioner is or is not the greatest analyst who ever lived in order to determine that it might have injured his reputation to be reported as having so proclaimed.

A self-condemnatory quotation may carry more force than criticism by another. It is against self-interest to admit one's own criminal liability, arrogance, or lack of integrity, and so all the more easy to credit when it happens. This principle underlies the elemental rule of evidence which permits the introduction of admissions, despite their hearsay character, because we assume "that persons do not make statements which are damaging to themselves unless satisfied for good reason that they are true."   [ ]

Of course, quotations do not always convey that the speaker actually said or wrote the quoted material. "Punctuation marks, like words, have many uses. Writers often use quotation marks, yet no reasonable reader would assume that such punctuation automatically implies the truth of the quoted material." *Baker v. Los Angeles Examiner*, 42 Cal. 3d, at 263, 721 P.2d, at 92. In *Baker*, a television reviewer printed a hypothetical conversation between a station vice president and writer/producer, and the court found that no reasonable reader would conclude the plaintiff in fact had made the statement attributed to him. [ ] Writers often use quotations as in *Baker*, and a reader will not reasonably understand the quotation to indicate reproduction of a conversation that took place. In other instances, an acknowledgement that the work is so-called docudrama or historical fiction or that it recreates conversations from memory, not from recordings, might indicate that the quotations should not be interpreted as the actual statements of the speaker to whom they are attributed.

The work at issue here, however, as with much journalistic writing, provides the reader no clue that the quotations are being used as a rhetorical device or to paraphrase the speaker's actual statements. To the contrary, the work purports to be nonfiction, the result of numerous interviews. At least a trier of fact could so conclude. The work contains lengthy quotations attributed to petitioner, and neither Malcolm nor her publishers indicate to the reader that the quotations are anything but the reproduction of actual conversations. Further, the work was published in The New Yorker, a magazine which at the relevant time seemed to enjoy a reputation for scrupulous factual accuracy. These factors would, or at least could, lead a reader to take the quotations at face value. A defendant may be able to argue to the jury that quotations should be viewed by the reader as nonliteral or reconstructions, but we conclude that a trier of fact in this case could find that the reasonable reader would understand the quotations to be nearly verbatim reports of statements made by the subject.

C

The constitutional question we must consider here is whether, in the framework of a summary judgment motion, the evidence suffices to show that respondents acted with the requisite knowledge of falsity or reckless disregard as to truth or falsity. This inquiry in turn requires us to consider the concept of falsity; for we cannot discuss the standards for knowledge or reckless disregard without some understanding of the acts required for liability. We must consider whether the requisite falsity inheres in the attribution of words to the petitioner which he did not speak.

In some sense, an alteration of a verbatim quotation is false. But writers and reporters by necessity alter what people say, at the very least to eliminate grammatical and syntactical infelicities. If every alteration constituted the falsity required to prove actual malice, the practice of journalism, which the First Amendment standard is designed to protect, would require a radical change, one inconsistent with our precedents and First Amendment principles. Petitioner concedes this absolute

definition of falsity in the quotation context is too
stringent, and acknowledges that "minor changes to
correct for grammar or syntax" do not amount to
falsity for purposes of proving actual malice. [ ]
We agree, and must determine what, in addition to this
technical falsity, proves falsity for purposes of the
actual malice inquiry.

Petitioner argues that, excepting correction of
grammar or syntax, publication of a quotation with
knowledge that it does not contain the words the
public figure used demonstrates actual malice. The
author will have published the quotation with
knowledge of falsity, and no more need be shown.
Petitioner suggests that by invoking more forgiving
standards the Court of Appeals would permit and
encourage the publication of falsehoods. Petitioner
believes that the intentional manufacture of
quotations does not "represen[t] the sort of
inaccuracy that is commonplace in the forum of robust
debate to which the *New York Times* rule applies,
[*Bose*], and that protection of deliberate falsehoods
would hinder the First Amendment values of robust and
well-informed public debate by reducing the
reliability of information available to the public.

We reject the idea that any alteration beyond
correction of grammar or syntax by itself proves
falsity in the sense relevant to determining actual
malice under the First Amendment. An interviewer who
writes from notes often will engage in the task of
attempting a reconstruction of the speaker's
statement. That author would, we may assume, act with
knowledge that at times she has attributed to her
subject words other than those actually used. Under
petitioner's proposed standard, an author in this
situation would lack First Amendment protection if she
reported as quotations the substance of a subjects
derogatory statements about himself.

Even if a journalist has tape recorded the spoken
statement of a public figure, the full and exact
statement will be reported in only rare circumstances.
The existence of both a speaker and a reporter; the
translation between two media, speech and the printed
word; the addition of punctuation; and the practical
necessity to edit and make intelligible a speaker's
perhaps rambling comments, all make it misleading to

suggest that a quotation will be reconstructed with complete accuracy. The use or absence of punctuation may distort a speaker's meaning, for example, where that meaning turns upon a speaker's emphasis of a particular word. In other cases, if a speaker makes an obvious misstatement, for example by unconscious substitution of one name for another, a journalist might alter the speaker's words but preserve his intended meaning. And conversely, an exact quotation out of context can distort meaning, although the speaker did use each reported word.

In all events, technical distinctions between correcting grammar and syntax and some greater level of alteration do not appear workable for we can think of no method by which courts or juries would draw the line between cleaning up and other changes, except by reference to the meaning a statement conveys to a reasonable reader. To attempt narrow distinctions of this type would be an unnecessary departure from First Amendment principles of general applicability, and, just as important, a departure from the underlying purposes of the tort of libel as understood since the latter half of the 16th century. From then until now, the tort action for defamation has existed to redress injury to the plaintiff's reputation by a statement that is defamatory and false. See [*Milkovich*]. As we have recognized, "[t]he legitimate state interest underlying the law of libel is the compensation of individuals for the harm inflicted on them by defamatory falsehood." [*Gertz*] If an author alters a speaker's words but effects no material change in meaning, including any meaning conveyed by the manner or fact of expression, the speaker suffers no injury to reputation that is compensable as a defamation.

These essential principles of defamation law accommodate the special cases of inaccurate quotations without the necessity for a discrete body of jurisprudence directed to this subject alone. Last Term, in [*Milkovich*], we refused "to create a wholesale defamation exemption for anything that might be labeled 'opinion.'" [ ] We recognized that "expressions of 'opinion' may often imply an assertion of objective fact." [ ] We allowed the defamation action to go forward in that case, holding that a reasonable trier of fact could find that the so-called expressions of opinion could be interpreted as including false assertions as to factual matters. So too in the case before us, we reject any special test of falsity for quotations, including one which would draw the line at correction of grammar or syntax. We conclude, rather, that the exceptions suggest by petitioner for grammatical or syntactical corrections serve to illuminate a broader principle.

The common law of libel takes but one approach to the question of falsity, regardless of the form of the communication. [ ] It overlooks minor inaccuracies and concentrates upon substantial truth. As in other jurisdictions, California law permits the defense of substantial truth, and would absolve a defendant even if she cannot "justify every word of the alleged defamatory matter; it is sufficient if the substance of the charge be proved true, irrespective of slight inaccuracy in the details." [ ] In this case, of course, the burden is upon petitioner to prove falsity. See [*Hepps*]. The essence of that inquiry, however, remains the same whether the burden rests upon plaintiff or defendant. Minor inaccuracies do not amount to falsity so long as "the substance, the gist, the sting, of the libelous change be justified." [ ] Put another way, the statement is not considered false unless it "would have a different effect on the mind of the reader from that which the pleaded truth would have produced." [ ] Our definition of actual malice relies upon this historical understanding.

We conclude that a deliberate alteration of the words uttered by a plaintiff does not equate with knowledge of falsity for purposes of [*New York Times* and *Gertz*], unless the alteration results in a material change in the meaning conveyed by statement. The use of quotations to attribute words not in fact spoken bears in a most important way on that inquiry, but it is not dispositive in every case.

Deliberate or reckless falsification that comprises actual malice turns upon words and punctuation only because words and punctuation express meaning. Meaning is the life of language. And, for the reasons we have given, quotations may be a devastating instrument for conveying false meaning. In the case under consideration, readers of In the Freud Archives may have found Malcolm's portrait of petitioner especially damning because so much of it appeared to be a self-portrait, told by petitioner in his own words. And if the alterations of petitioner's words gave a different meaning to the statements, bearing upon their defamatory character,, then the device of quotations might well be critical in finding the words actionable.

D

The Court of Appeals applied a test of substantial truth which, in exposition if not in application, comports with much of the above discussion. The Court of Appeals, however, went one step beyond protection of quotations that convey the meaning of a speaker's statement with substantial accuracy and concluded '"that an altered quotation is protected so long as it is a "rational interpretation" of an actual statement drawing this standard from our decisions in Time, Inc. v. Pape, 401 U. S. 279 (1971), and [Bose]. Application of our protection for rational interpretation in this context finds no support in general principles of defamation law or in our First Amendment jurisprudence. Neither *Time, Inc. v. Pape*, nor *Bose Corp.*, involved the fabrication of quotations, or any analogous claim, and because many of the quotations at issue might reasonably be construed to state or imply factual assertions that are both false and defamatory, we cannot accept the reasoning of the Court of Appeals on this point.

In *Time, Inc. v. Pape,* we reversed a libel judgment which arose out of a magazine article summarizing a report by the United States Commission on Civil Rights discussing police civil rights abuses. The article quoted the Commission's summary of facts surrounding an incident of police brutality, but failed to include the Commission's qualification that these were allegations taken from a civil complaint. The Court noted that "the attitude of the Commission toward the factual verity of the episodes recounted was anything but straightforward," and distinguished between a "direct account of events that speak for themselves," 401 U. S., at 285, 286, and an article descriptive of what the Commission had reported. *Time, Inc. v. Pape* took into account the difficult choices that confront an author who departs from direct quotation and offers his own interpretation of an ambiguous source. A fair reading of our opinion is that the defendant did not publish a falsification sufficient to sustain a finding of actual malice.

In *Bose Corp.*, a Consumer Reports reviewer had attempted to describe in words the experience of listening to music through a pair of loudspeakers, and we concluded that the result was not an assessment of events that speak for themselves, but "'one of a number of possible rational interpretations' of an event 'that bristled with ambiguities' and descriptive challenges for the writer." [ ] We refused to permit recovery for choice of language which, though perhaps reflecting a misconception, represented "the sort of inaccuracy that is commonplace in the forum of robust debate to which the *New York Times* rule applies." [ ]

The protection for rational interpretation serves First Amendment principles by allowing an author the interpretive license that is necessary when relying upon ambiguous sources. Where, however, a writer uses a quotation, and where a reasonable reader would conclude that the quotation purports to be a verbatim repetition of a statement by the speaker, the quotation marks indicate that the author is not involved in an interpretation of the speaker's ambiguous statement, but attempting to convey what the speaker said. This orthodox use of a quotation is the quintessential "direct account of events that speak for themselves." *Time, Inc. v. Pape, supra,* at 285. More accurately, the quotation allows the subject to speak for himself.

The significance of the quotations at issue, absent any qualification, is to inform us that we are reading the statement of petitioner, not Malcolm's rational interpretation of what petitioner has said or thought. Were we to assess quotations under a rational interpretation standard, we would give journalists the freedom to place statements in their subjects' mouths without fear of liability. By eliminating any method of distinguishing between the statements of the subject and the interpretation of the author, we would diminish to a great degree the trustworthiness of the printed word, and eliminate the real meaning of quotations. Not only public figures but the press doubtless would suffer under such a rule. Newsworthy figures might become more wary of journalists, knowing that any comment could be transmuted and attributed to the subject, so long as some bounds of rational interpretation were not exceeded. We would ill serve the values of the First Amendment if we were to grant near absolute, constitutional protection for such a practice. We doubt the suggestion that as a general rule readers will assume that direct quotations are but a rational interpretation of the speaker's words, and we decline to adopt any such presumption in determining the permissible interpretations of the quotations in question here.

III

A

We apply these principles to the case before us. On summary judgment, we must draw all justifiable inferences in favor of the nonmoving party, including questions of credibility and of the weight to be accorded particular evidence. [*Liberty Lobby*] So we must assume, except where otherwise evidenced by the transcripts of the tape recordings, that petitioner is correct in denying that he made the statements attributed to him by Malcolm, and that Malcolm reported with knowledge or reckless disregard of the differences between what petitioner said and what was quoted.

Respondents argue that, in determining whether petitioner has shown sufficient falsification to survive summary judgment, we should consider not only the tape recorded statements but also Malcolm's typewritten notes. We must decline that suggestion. To begin with, petitioner affirms in an affidavit that he did not make the complained of statements. The record contains substantial additional evidence, moreover, evidence which, in a light most favorable to petitioner, would support a jury determination under a clear and convincing standard that Malcolm deliberately or recklessly altered the quotations.

First, many of the challenged passages resemble quotations that appear on the tapes, except for the addition or alteration of certain phrases, giving rise to a reasonable inference that the statements have been altered. Second, Malcolm had the tapes in her possession and was not working under a tight deadline.

Unlike a case involving hot news, Malcolm cannot complain that she lacked the practical ability to compare the tapes with her work in progress. Third, Malcolm represented to the editor-in-chief of The New Yorker that all the quotations were from the tape recordings. Fourth, Malcolm's explanations of the time and place of unrecorded conversations during which petitioner allegedly made some of the quoted statements have not been consistent in all respects. Fifth, petitioner suggests that the progression from typewritten notes, to manuscript, then to galleys provides further evidence of intentional alteration. Malcolm contests petitioner's allegations, and only a trial on the merits will resolve the factual dispute. But at this stage, the evidence creates a jury question whether Malcolm published the statements with knowledge or reckless disregard of the alterations.

B

We must determine whether the published passages differ materially in meaning from the tape recorded statements so as to create an issue of fact for a jury as to falsity.

(a) *"Intellectual Gigolo."* We agree with the dissenting opinion in the Court of Appeals that "[f]airly read, intellectual gigolo suggests someone who forsakes intellectual integrity in exchange for pecuniary or other gain." [ ] A reasonable jury could find a material difference between the meaning of this passage and petitioner's tape-recorded statement that he was considered "much too junior within the hierarchy of analysis, for these important training analysts to be caught dead with [him]."

The Court of Appeals majority found it difficult to perceive how the "intellectual gigolo" quotation was defamatory, a determination supported not by any citation to California law, but only by the argument that the passage appears to be a report of Eissler's and Anna Freud's opinions of petitioner. [ ] We agree with the Court of Appeals that the most natural interpretation of this quotation is not an admission that petitioner considers himself an intellectual gigolo but a statement that Eissler and Anna Freud considered him so. It does not follow, though, that the statement is harmless. Petitioner is entitled to argue that the passage should be analyzed as if Malcolm had reported falsely that *Eissler* had given this assessment (with the added level of complexity that the quotation purports to represent petitioner's understanding of Eissler's view). An admission that two well-respected senior colleagues considered one an "intellectual gigolo" could be as or more damaging than a similar self-appraisal. In all events, whether the "intellectual gigolo" quotation is defamatory is a question of California law. To the extent that the Court of Appeals bases its conclusion in the First Amendment, it was mistaken.

The Court of Appeals relied upon the "incremental harm" doctrine as an alternative basis for its decision. As the court explained it, "[t]his doctrine measures the incremental reputational harm inflicted by the challenged statements beyond the harm imposed by the nonactionable remainder of the publication." [ ] The court ruled, as a matter of law, that "[g]iven the...many provocative, bombastic statements indisputably made by Masson and quoted by Malcolm, the additional harm caused by the 'intellectual gigolo' quote was nominal or nonexistent, rendering the defamation claim as to this quote nonactionable." [ ]

This reasoning requires a court to conclude that, in fact, a plaintiff made the other quoted statements, cf. [*Liberty Lobby*]. As noted by the dissent in the Court of Appeals, the most "provocative, bombastic statements" quoted by Malcolm are those complained of by petitioner, and so this would not seem an appropriate application of the incremental harm doctrine. 895 F. 2d, at 1566.

(b) *"Sex, Women, Fun."* This passage presents a closer question. The "sex, women, fun" quotation offers a very different picture of petitioner's plans for Maresfield Gardens than his remark that "Freud's library alone is priceless." [ ] Petitioner's other tape-recorded remarks did indicate that he and another analyst planned to have great parties at the Freud house and, in a context that may not even refer to Freud house activities, to "pass women on to each other." We cannot conclude as a matter of law that these remarks bear the same substantial meaning as the quoted passage's suggestion that petitioner would make the Freud house a place of "sex, women, fun."

(c)   *"It Sounded Better."*   We agree with the District and the Court of Appeals that any difference between petitioner's tape-recorded statement that he "just liked" the name Moussaieff, and the quotation that "it sounded better" is, in context, immaterial. Although Malcolm did not include all of petitioner's lengthy explanation of his name change, she did convey the gist of that explanation: Petitioner took his abandoned family name as his middle name. We agree with the Court of Appeals that the words attributed to petitioner did not materially alter the meaning of his statement.

(d)   *"I Don't Know Why I Put It In."*   Malcolm quotes petitioner as saying that he "tacked on at the last minute" a "totally gratuitous" remark about the "sterility of psychoanalysis" in an academic paper, and that he did so for no particular reason. In the tape recordings, petitioner does admit that the remark was "possibly [a] gratuitously offensive way to end a paper to a group of analysts," but when asked why he included the remark, he answered "[because] it was true...I really believe it."   Malcolm's version contains material differences from petitioner's statement, and it is conceivable that the alteration results in a statement that could injure a scholar's reputation.

(e)   *"Greatest Analyst Who Ever Lived."*   While petitioner did, on numerous occasions, predict that his theories would do irreparable damage to the practice of psychoanalysis, and did suggest that no other analyst shared his views, no tape-recorded statement appears to contain the substance or the arrogant and unprofessional tone apparent in this quotation. A material difference exists between the quotation and the tape-recorded statements, and a jury could find that the difference exposed petitioner to contempt, ridicule or obloquy.

(f)   *"He Had The Wrong Man."*   The quoted version makes it appear as if petitioner rejected a plea to remain in stoic silence and do "the honorable thing." The tape-recorded version indicates that petitioner rejected a plea supported by far more varied motives: Eissler told petitioner that not only would silence be "the honorable thing," but petitioner would "save face." and might be rewarded for that silence with eventual reinstatement. Petitioner described himself as willing to undergo a scandal in order to shine the light of publicity upon the actions of the Freud Archives, while Malcolm would have petitioner describe himself as a person who was "the wrong man" to do "the honorable thing." This difference is material, a jury might find it defamatory, and, for the reasons we have given, there is evidence to support a finding of deliberate or reckless falsification.

C

Because of the Court of Appeals' disposition with respect to Malcolm, it did not have occasion to address petitioner's argument that the District Court erred in granting summary judgment to The New Yorker Magazine, Inc., and Alfred A. Knopf, Inc. on the basis of their respective relations with Malcolm or the lack of any independent actual malice. These questions are best addressed in the first instance on remand.

The judgment of the Court of Appeals is reversed, and the case is remanded for further proceedings consistent with this opinion.

It is so ordered.

JUSTICE WHITE, with whom JUSTICE SCALIA joins, concurring in part and dissenting in part.

. . .

As this case comes to us, it is to be judged on the basis that in the instances identified by the court, the reporter, Malcolm, wrote that Masson said certain things that she knew Masson did not say. By any definition of the term, this was "knowing falsehood" Malcolm asserts that Masson said these very words, knowing that he did not. The issue, as the Court recognizes, is whether Masson spoke the words attributed to him, not whether the fact, if any, asserted by the attributed words is true or false. In my view, we need to go no further to conclude that the defendants in this case were not entitled to summary judgment on the issue of malice with respect to any of the six erroneous quotations.

That there was at least an issue for the jury to decide on the question of deliberate or reckless falsehood, does not mean that plaintiffs were necessarily entitled to go to trial. If, as a matter of law, reasonable jurors could not conclude that attributing to Masson certain words that he did not say amounted to libel under California law, i.e., "expose[d] [Masson] to hatred, contempt, ridicule, or obloquy, or which causes him to be shunned or avoided, or which has a tendency to injure him in his occupation," [ ] a motion for summary judgment on this ground would be justified. I would suppose, for example, that if Malcolm wrote that Masson said that he wore contact lenses, when he said nothing about his eyes or his vision, the trial judge would grant summary judgment for the defendants and dismiss the case. The same would be true if Masson had said "I was spoiled as a child by my Mother," whereas, Malcolm reports that he said "I was spoiled as a child by my parents." But if reasonable jurors should conclude that the deliberate misquotation was libelous, the case should go to the jury.

This seems to me to be the straightforward, traditional approach to deal with this case. Instead, the Court states that deliberate misquotation does not amount to *New York Times* malice unless it results in a material change in the meaning conveyed by the statement. This ignores the fact that under *New York Times*, reporting a known falsehood--here the knowingly false attribution--is sufficient proof of malice. The falsehood, apparently, must be substantial; the reporter may lie a little, but not too much.

This standard is not only a less manageable one than the traditional approach, but it also assigns to the courts issues that are for the jury to decide. For a court to ask whether a misquotation substantially alters the meaning of spoken words in a defamatory manner is a far different inquiry than whether reasonable jurors could find that the misquotation was different enough to be libelous. In the one case, the court is measuring the difference from its own point of view; in the other it is asking how the jury would or could view the erroneous attribution.

The Court attempts to justify its holding in several ways, none of which is persuasive. First, it observes that an interviewer who takes notes of any interview will attempt to reconstruct what the speaker said and will often knowingly attribute to the subject words that were not used by the speaker. [ ] But this is nothing more than an assertion that authors may misrepresent because they cannot remember what the speaker actually said. This should be no dilemma for such authors, or they could report their story without purporting to quote when they are not sure, thereby leaving the reader to trust or doubt the author rather than believing that the subject actually said what he is claimed to have said. Moreover, this basis for the Court's rule has no application where there is a tape of the interview and the author is in no way at a loss to know what the speaker actually said. Second, the Court speculates that even with the benefit of a recording, the author will find it necessary at times to reconstruct, [ ] but again, in those cases why should the author be free to put his or her reconstruction in quotation marks, rather than report without them? Third, the Court suggests that misquotations that do not materially alter the meaning inflict no injury to reputation that is compensable as defamation. [ ] This may be true, but this is a question of defamation or not, and has nothing to do with whether the author deliberately put within quotation marks and attributed to the speaker words that the author knew the speaker did not utter.

As I see it, the defendants' motion for summary judgment based on lack of malice should not have been granted on any of the six quotations considered by the Court in Part III-B of its opinion. I therefore dissent from the result reached with respect to the "It Sounded Better" quotation dealt with in paragraph (c) of Part III-B, but agree with the Court's judgment on the other five misquotations.

Notes and Questions

1.   Suppose at trial the jury finds (1) that the "intellectual gigolo" quote deliberately and materially altered the meaning of what Masson actually said, but that the resulting misquotation was not defamatory; (2) other passages in the article were false and defamatory, but there was no evidence that

Malcolm knew those were false or had serious doubts as to their truth. Would these findings meet the Court's requirement that there be a deliberate alteration that "results in a material change in the meaning conveyed by the statement"? Why did the Court stop short of requiring a finding that the changed meaning is defamatory? Does its analysis of specific quotations suggest that the latter is in fact the test?

2. The district court held that even if Malcolm could be held liable, the *New Yorker* and the book publisher could not because Malcolm's actual malice, if any, could not be attributed to them. Neither the Court of Appeals nor the Supreme Court considered that issue. Principles of *respondeat superior* may make an employer liable for the actual malice of an employee (see *Cantrell*), but Malcolm apparently was a freelancer.

3. In a case described as the "mirror image" of *Masson* a petition for certiorari has been filed in Diesen v. Hessburg (No. 90-854). Donald Diesen, a former county attorney, claims to have been libeled by articles in the *Duluth News-Tribune* concerning his record in prosecuting cases of domestic abuse. Diesen told the court in his petition for certiorari that *Masson* involved the issue of allegedly defamatory statements in which the gist is right but the details wrong, and that his case involves a question of getting the details right but the gist wrong. Although a trial court jury awarded Diesen a total of $785,000 in damages, the Minnesota Supreme Court had reversed, 17 Med.L.Rptr. 1849), holding that true statements, or statements of opinion on matters of public concern, cannot give rise to a cause of action for defamation by implication. Med.L.Rptr., News Notes, Jan. 29, 1991.

Add to casebook p. 586, after 2nd full paragraph:

On June 26, 1989, the Supreme Court affirmed the $6 million award, holding that the Excessive Fines Clause does not apply to awards of punitive damages between private parties, although it left open the possibility of a challenge to excessive punitive awards under the Fourteenth Amendment's Due Process Clause. Browning-Ferris Industries of Vermont Inc. v. Kelco Disposal Inc., 109 S.Ct. 2909 (1989). A few days later it denied *certiorari* in a libel case in which the newspaper had been held liable for punitive damages of $2 million. DiSalle v. P.G. Publishing Co., 375 Pa.Super. 510, 544 A.2d 1345, 15 Med.L.Rptr. 1873 (1988), certiorari denied 109 S.Ct. 3216 (1989).

Other examples of megaverdicts include a jury award of $34 million (to be appealed) to an attorney who sued *The Philadelphia Inquirer* for libel after it alleged improprieties in his conduct as a prosecutor, Sprague v. Philadelphia Newspapers, Inc., Med.L.Rptr., News Notes, May 15, 1990, and a $29 million libel and invasion of privacy verdict (to be appealed) against a television station for reports concerning the suspension of a doctor's medical privileges by two hospitals, Srivastava v. Harte-Hanks Television, Inc., Med.L.Rptr., News Notes, May 29, 1990. In the latter case, the jury awarded the plaintiff $1.75 million for loss of earnings from his medical practice in the past, $5 million for mental anguish in the past, $500,000 for mental anguish in the future, $1.5 million for loss of reputation in the future, and $17.5 million in exemplary damages.

Chapter XIII

PRIVACY

Add to casebook p. 623, after note 8:

9. The Supreme Court of the United States decided the *Florida Star* case in June 1989.

THE FLORIDA STAR v. B.J.F.
Supreme Court of the United States, 1989.
491 U.S. 524, 109 S.Ct. 2608, 105 L.Ed.2d 443,
16 Med.L.Rptr. 1801.

JUSTICE MARSHALL delivered the opinion of the Court.

Florida Stat. § 794.03 (1987) makes it unlawful to "print, publish, or broadcast . . . in any instrument of mass communication" the name of the victim of a sexual offense. Pursuant to this statute, appellant The Florida Star was found civilly liable for publishing the name of a rape victim which it had obtained from a publicly released police report. The issue presented here is whether this result comports with the First Amendment. We hold that it does not.

I

The Florida Star is a weekly newspaper which serves the community of Jacksonville, Florida, and which has an average circulation of approximately 18,000 copies. A regular feature of the newspaper is its "Police Reports" section. That section, typically two to three pages in length, contains brief articles describing local criminal incidents under police investigation.

On October 20, 1983, appellee B.J.F. reported to the Duval County, Florida, Sheriff's Department (the Department) that she had been robbed and sexually assaulted by an unknown assailant. The Department prepared a report on the incident which identified B.J.F., by her full name. The Department then placed the report in its press room. The Department does not restrict access either to the press room or to the reports made available therein.

A Florida Star reporter-trainee sent to the press room copied the police report verbatim, including B.J.F.'s full name, on a blank duplicate of the Department's forms. A Florida Star reporter then prepared a one-paragraph article about the crime, derived entirely from the trainee's copy of the police report. The article included B.J.F.'s full name. It appeared in the "Robberies" subsection of the "Police Reports" section on October 29, 1983, one of fifty-four police blotter stories in that day's edition. The article read:

> "[B.J.F.] reported on Thursday, October 20, she was crossing Brentwood Park, which is in the 500 block of Golfair Boulevard, enroute to her bus stop, when an unknown black man ran up behind the lady and placed a knife to her neck and told her not to yell. The suspect then undressed the lady and had sexual intercourse with her before fleeing the scene with her 60 cents, Timex watch and gold necklace. Patrol efforts have been suspended concerning this incident because of a lack of evidence."

In printing B.J.F.'s full name, The Florida Star violated its internal policy of not publishing the names of sexual offense victims.

On September 26, 1984, B.J.F. filed suit in the Circuit Court of Duval County against the Department and The Florida Star, alleging that these parties negligently violated § 794.03. Before trial, the Department settled with B.J.F. for $2,500. The Florida Star moved to dismiss, claiming, *inter alia*, that imposing civil sanctions on the newspaper pursuant to § 794.03 violated the First Amendment. The trial judge rejected the motion. [ ]

At the ensuing day-long trial, B.J.F. testified that she had suffered emotional distress from the publication of her name. She stated that she had heard about the article from fellow workers and acquaintances; that her mother had received several threatening phone calls from a man who stated that he would rape B.J.F. again; and that these events had forced B.J.F. to change her phone number and residence, to seek police protection, and to obtain mental health counseling. In defense, The Florida

Star put forth evidence indicating that the newspaper had learned B.J.F.'s name from the incident report released by the Department, and that the newspaper's violation of its internal rule against publishing the names of sexual offense victims was inadvertent.

At the close of B.J.F.'s case, and again at the close of its defense, The Florida Star moved for a directed verdict. On both occasions, the trial judge denied these motions. He ruled from the bench that § 794.03 was constitutional because it reflected a proper balance between the First Amendment and privacy rights, as it applied only to a narrow set of "rather sensitive . . . criminal offenses." [ ] At the close of [the newspaper's] defense, the judge granted B.J.F.'s motion for a directed verdict on the issue of negligence, finding the newspaper *per se* negligent based upon its violation of § 794.03. [ ]   This ruling left the jury to consider only the questions of causation and damages. The judge instructed the jury that it could award B.J.F. punitive damages if it found that the newspaper had "acted with reckless indifference to the rights of others." [ ] The jury awarded B.J.F. $75,000 in compensatory damages and $25,000 in punitive damages. Against the actual damage award, the judge set off B.J.F.'s settlement with the Department.

The First District Court of Appeal affirmed in a three-paragraph *per curiam* opinion. [ ]   In the paragraph devoted to the Florida Star's First Amendment claim, the court stated that the directed verdict for B.J.F. had been properly entered because, under § 794.03, a rape victim's name is "of a private nature and not to be published as a matter of law." [ ] The Supreme Court of Florida denied discretionary review.

The Florida Star appealed to this court. We noted probable jurisdiction, [ ], and now reverse.

II

The tension between the right which the First Amendment accords to a free press, on the one hand, and the protections which various statutes and common-law doctrines accord to personal privacy against the publication of truthful information, on the other, is a subject we have addressed several times in recent years. Our decisions in cases involving government attempts to sanction the accurate dissemination of information as invasive of privacy, have not, however, exhaustively considered this conflict. On the contrary, although our decisions have without exception upheld the press' right to publish, we have emphasized each time that we were resolving this conflict only as it arose in a discrete factual context.

The parties to this case frame their contentions in light of a trilogy of cases which have presented, in different contexts, the conflict between truthful reporting and state-protected privacy interests. In [*Cox*], we found unconstitutional a civil damages award entered against a television station for broadcasting the name of a rape-murder victim which the station had obtained from courthouse records. In *Oklahoma Publishing Co. v. District Court*, 430 U.S. 308 [2 Med.L.Rptr. 1456] (1977), we found unconstitutional a state court's pretrial order enjoining the media from publishing the name or photograph of an 11-year-old boy in connection with a juvenile proceeding involving that child which reporters had attended. Finally, in [*Smith v. Daily Mail*, p. 27 (the casebook), *supra*], we found unconstitutional the indictment of two newspapers for violating a state statute forbidding newspapers to publish, without written approval of the juvenile court, the name of any youth charged as a juvenile offender. The papers had learned about a shooting by monitoring a police band radio frequency, and had obtained the name of the alleged juvenile assailant from witnesses, the police, and a local prosecutor.

Appellant takes the position that this case is indistinguishable from [*Cox*]. [ ] Alternatively, it urges that our decisions in the above trilogy, and in other cases in which we have held that the right of the press to publish truth overcame asserted interests other than personal privacy, can be distilled to yield a broader First Amendment principle that the press may never be punished, civilly or criminally, for publishing the truth. [ ] Appellee counters that the privacy trilogy is inapposite, because in each case the private information already appeared on a "public record," [ ], and because the privacy interests at

stake were far less profound than in the present case.
[ ] In the alternative, appellee urges that [Cox] be
overruled and replaced with a categorical rule that
publication of the name of a rape victim never enjoys
constitutional protection. [ ]

We conclude that imposing damages on appellant
for publishing B.J.F.'s name violates the First
Amendment, although not for either of the reasons
appellant urges. Despite the strong resemblance this
case bears to [Cox], that case cannot fairly be read
as controlling here. The name of the rape victim in
that case was obtained from courthouse records that
were open to public inspection . . .. [ ]
Significantly, one of the reasons we gave in [Cox] for
invalidating the challenged damages award was the
important role the press plays in subjecting trials to
public scrutiny and thereby helping guarantee their
fairness. [ ] That role is not directly compromised
where, as here, the information in question comes from
a police report prepared and disseminated at a time at
which not only had no adversarial criminal proceedings
begun, but no suspect had been identified.

Nor need we accept appellant's invitation to hold
broadly that truthful publication may never be
punished consistent with the First Amendment. Our
cases have carefully eschewed reaching this ultimate
question, mindful that the future may bring scenarios
which prudence counsels our not resolving
anticipatorily. [ ] Indeed, in [Cox], we pointedly
refused to answer even the less sweeping question
"whether truthful publications may ever be subjected
to civil or criminal liability" for invading "an area
of privacy" defined by the State. [ ] Respecting the
fact that press freedom and privacy rights are both
"plainly rooted in the traditions and significant
concerns of our society," we instead focused on the
less sweeping issue of "whether the State may impose
sanctions on the accurate publication of the name of
a rape victim obtained from public records--more
specifically, from judicial records which are
maintained in connection with a public prosecution and
which themselves are open to public inspection." [ ]
We continue to believe that the sensitivity and
significance of the interests presented in clashes
between First Amendment and privacy rights counsel
relying on limited principles that sweep no more

broadly than the appropriate context of the instant case.

In our view, this case is appropriately analyzed with reference to such a limited First Amendment principle.   It is the one, in fact, which we articulated in *Daily Mail* in our synthesis of prior cases involving attempts to punish truthful publication: "[I]f a newspaper lawfully obtains truthful information about a matter of public significance then state officials may not constitutionally punish publication of the information, absent a need to further a state interest of the highest order."   [ ]   According the press the ample protection provided by that principle is supported by at least three separate considerations, in addition to, of course, the overarching "'public interest, secured by the Constitution, in the dissemination of truth.'"   [ ]   The cases on which the *Daily Mail* synthesis relied demonstrate these considerations.

First, because the *Daily Mail* formulation only protects the publication of information which a newspaper has "lawfully obtain[ed]," [ ], the government retains ample means of safeguarding significant interests upon which publication may impinge, including protecting a rape victim's anonymity. To the extent sensitive information rests in private hands, the government may under some circumstances forbid its nonconsensual acquisition, thereby bringing outside of the *Daily Mail* principle the publication of any information so acquired. To the extent sensitive information is in the government's custody, it has even greater power to forestall or mitigate the injury caused by its release.   The government may classify certain information, establish and enforce procedures ensuring its redacted release, and extend a damages remedy against the government or its officials where the government's mishandling of sensitive information leads to its dissemination.   Where information is entrusted to the government, a less drastic means than punishing truthful publication almost always exists for guarding against the dissemination of private facts. [ ]

A second consideration undergirding the *Daily Mail* principle is the fact that punishing the press for its dissemination of information which is already publicly available is relatively unlikely to advance the interests in the service of which the State seeks to act.   It is not, of course, always the case that information lawfully acquired by the press is known, or accessible, to others.   But where the government has made certain information publicly available, it is highly anomalous to sanction persons other than the source of its release.   We noted this anomaly in [*Cox*]:   "By placing the information in the public domain on official court records, the State must be presumed to have concluded that the public interest was thereby being served."   [ ]   The *Daily Mail* formulation reflects the fact that it is a limited set of cases indeed where, despite the accessibility of the public to certain information, a meaningful public interest is served by restricting its further release by other entities, like the press.   As *Daily Mail* observed in its summary of *Oklahoma Publishing*, "once the truthful information was 'publicly revealed' or 'in the public domain' the court could not constitutionally restrain its dissemination."   [ ]

A third and final consideration is the "timidity and self-censorship" which may result from allowing the media to be punished for publishing certain truthful information.   [ ]   [*Cox*] noted this concern with overdeterrence in the context of information made public through official court records, but the fear of excessive media self-suppression is inapplicable as well to other information released, without qualification, by the government.   A contrary rule, depriving protection to those who rely on the government's implied representations of the lawfulness of dissemination, would force upon the media the onerous obligation of sifting through government press releases, reports, and pronouncements to prune out material arguably unlawful for publication.   This situation could inhere even where the newspaper's sole object was to reproduce, with no substantial change, the government's rendition of the event in question.

Applied to the instant case, the *Daily Mail* principle clearly commands reversal.   The first inquiry is whether the newspaper "lawfully obtain[ed] truthful information about a matter of public

significance."   [ ]   It is undisputed that the news
article describing the assault on B.J.F. was accurate.
In addition, appellant lawfully obtained B.J.F.'s
name. Appellee's argument to the contrary is based on
the fact that under Florida law, police reports which
reveal the identity of the victim of a sexual offense
are not among the matters of "public record" which the
public, by law, is entitled to inspect. [ ] But the
fact that state officials are not required to disclose
such reports does not make it unlawful for a newspaper
to receive them when furnished by the government. Nor
does the fact that the Department apparently failed to
fulfill its obligation under § 794.03 not to "cause or
allow to be . . . published" the name of a sexual
offense victim make the newspaper's ensuing receipt of
this   information   unlawful.   Even   assuming   the
Constitution permitted a State to proscribe *receipt* of
information, Florida has not taken this step. It is
clear, furthermore, that the news article concerned "a
matter of public significance," [ ], in the sense in
which the *Daily Mail* synthesis of prior cases used
that term. That is, the article generally, as opposed
to the specific identity contained within it, involved
a matter of paramount public import: the commission,
and investigation, of a violent crime which had been
reported to authorities. [ ]

The second inquiry is whether imposing liability
on appellant pursuant to § 794.03 serves "a need to
further a state interest of the highest order."   [ ]
Appellee argues that a rule punishing publication
furthers three closely related interests: the privacy
of victims of sexual offenses; the physical safety of
such victims, who may be targeted for retaliation if
their names become known to their assailants; and the
goal of encouraging victims of such crimes to report
these offenses without fear of exposure. [ ]

At a time in which we are daily reminded of the
tragic reality of rape, it is undeniable that these
are highly significant interests, a fact underscored
by the Florida Legislature's explicit attempt to
protect these interests by enacting a criminal statute
prohibiting much dissemination of victim identifies.
We accordingly do not rule out the possibility that,
in a proper case, imposing civil sanctions for
publication of the name of a rape victim might be so
overwhelmingly necessary to advance these interests as

to satisfy the *Daily Mail* standard.   For three
independent reasons, however, imposing liability for
publication under the circumstances of this case is
too precipitous a means of advancing these interests
to convince us that there is a "need" within the
meaning of the *Daily Mail* formulation for Florida to
take this extreme step.   [ ]

     First is the manner in which appellant obtained
the identifying information in question. As we have
noted,   where   the   government   itself   provides
information to the media, it is most appropriate to
assume that the government had, but failed to utilize,
far   more   limited   means   of   guarding   against
dissemination than the extreme step of punishing
truthful speech. That assumption is richly borne out
in this case. B.J.F.'s identity would never have come
to   light   were   it   not   for   the   erroneous,   if
inadvertent, inclusion by the Department of her full
name in an incident report made available in a press
room open to the public.   Florida's policy against
disclosure of rape victims' identifies, reflected in
§ 794.03, was undercut by the Department's failure to
abide by this policy. Where, as here, the government
has   failed   to   police   itself   in   disseminating
information, it is clear under [*Cox*], *Oklahoma
Publishing*, and *Landmark Communications* that the
imposition of damages against the press for its
subsequent publication can hardly be said to be a
narrowly tailored means of safeguarding anonymity.
[ ]   Once the government has placed such information
in the public domain, "reliance must rest upon the
judgment of those who decide what to publish or
broadcast," [ ], and hopes for restitution must rest
upon the willingness of the government to compensate
victims for their loss of privacy, and to protect them
from the other consequences of its mishandling of the
information   which   these   victims   provided   in
confidence.

     That appellant gained access to the information
in question through a government news release made it
especially likely that, if liability were to be
imposed, self-censorship would result. Reliance on a
news release is a paradigmatically "routine newspaper
reporting techniqu[e]."   [ ]   The government's
issuance of such a release, without qualification, an
only   convey   to   recipients   that   the   government

considered dissemination lawful, and indeed expected
the recipients to disseminate the information further.
Had appellant merely reproduced the news release
prepared and released by the Department, imposing
civil damages would surely violate the First
Amendment.   The fact that appellant converted the
police report into a news story by adding the
linguistic connecting tissue necessary to transform
the report's facts into full sentences cannot change
this result.

A second problem with Florida's imposition of
liability for publication is the broad sweep of the
negligence *per se* standard applied under the civil
cause of action implied from § 794.03. Unlike claims
based on the common law tort of invasion of privacy,
[ ], civil actions based on § 794.03 require no case-
by-case findings that the disclosure of a fact about
a person's private life was one that a reasonable
person would find highly offensive. On the contrary,
under the *per se* theory of negligence adopted by the
courts below, liability follows automatically from
publication.   This is so regardless of whether the
identity of the victim has otherwise become a
reasonable subject of public concern--because,
perhaps, questions have arisen whether the victim
fabricated an assault by a particular person. Nor is
there a scienter requirement of any kind under
§ 794.03, engendering the perverse result that
truthful publications challenged pursuant to this
cause of action are less protected by the First
Amendment than even the least protected defamatory
falsehoods: those involving purely private figures,
where liability is evaluated under a standard, usually
applied by a jury, of ordinary negligence. [ ] We
have previously noted the impermissibility of
categorical prohibitions upon media access where
important First Amendment interests are at stake. [ ]
More individualized adjudication is no less
indispensable where the State, seeking to safeguard
the anonymity of crime victims, sets its face against
publication of their names.

Third, and finally, the facial underinclusiveness
of § 794.03 raises serious doubts about whether
Florida is, in fact, serving, with this statute, the
significant interests which appellee invokes in
support of affirmance. Section 794.03 prohibits the

publication of identifying information only if this information appears in an "instrument of mass communication," a term the statute does not define. Section 794.03 does not prohibit the spread by other means of the identities of victims of sexual offenses. An individual who maliciously spreads word of the identity of a rape victim is thus not covered, despite the fact that the communication of such information to persons who live near, or work with, the victim may have consequences equally devastating as the exposure of her name to large numbers of strangers. [ ]

When a State attempts the extraordinary measure of punishing truthful publication in the name of privacy, it must demonstrate its commitment to advancing this interest by applying its prohibition evenhandedly, to the smalltime disseminator as well as the media giant. Where important First Amendment interests are at stake, the mass scope of disclosure is not an acceptable surrogate for injury. A ban on disclosures effected by "instrument[s] of mass communication" simply cannot be defended on the ground that partial prohibitions may effect partial relief. [ ] Without more careful and inclusive precautions against alternative forms of dissemination, we cannot conclude that Florida's selective ban on publication by the mass media satisfactorily accomplishes its stated purpose.

III

Our holding today is limited. We do not hold that truthful publication is automatically constitutionally protected, or that there is no zone of personal privacy within which the State may protect the individual from intrusion by the press, or even that a State may never punish publication of the name of a victim of a sexual offense. We hold only that where a newspaper publishes truthful information which it has lawfully obtained, punishment may lawfully be imposed, if at all, only when narrowly tailored to a state interest of the highest order, and that no such interest is satisfactorily served by imposing liability under § 794.03 to appellant under the facts of this case. The decision below is therefore

Reversed.

Justice Scalia, concurring in part and concurring in the judgment.

I think it is sufficient to decide this case to rely upon the third ground set forth in the Court's opinion, [ ]: that a law cannot be regarded as protecting an interest "of the highest order," [ ] and thus as justifying a restriction upon truthful speech, when it leaves appreciable damage to that supposedly vital interest unprohibited. In the present case, I would anticipate that the rape victim's discomfort at the dissemination of news of her misfortune among friends and acquaintances would be at least as great as her discomfort at its publication by the media to people to whom she is only a name. . . .

This law has every appearance of a prohibition that society is prepared to impose upon the press but not upon itself. Such a prohibition does not protect an interest "of the highest order." For that reason, I agree that the judgment of the court below must be reversed.

Justice White, with whom The Chief Justice and Justice O'Connor join, dissenting.

"Short of homicide, [rape] is the 'ultimate violation of self.'" [ ] For B.J.F., however, the violation she suffered at a rapist's knifepoint marked only the beginning of her ordeal. A week later, while her assailant was still at large, an account of this assault--identifying by name B.J.F. as the victim--was published by The Florida Star. As a result, B.J.F. received harassing phone calls, required mental health counseling, was forced to move from her home, and was even threatened with being raped again. Yet today, the Court holds that a jury award of $75,000 to compensate B.J.F. for the harm she suffered due to the Star's negligence is at odds with the First Amendment. I do not accept this result.

The Court reaches its conclusion based on an analysis of three of our precedents and a concern with three particular aspects of the judgment against appellant. I consider each of these points in turn, and then consider some of the larger issues implicated by today's decision.

                                I

    The Court finds its result compelled, or at least
supported in varying degrees, by three of our prior
cases: [*Cox, Oklahoma Publishing, Daily Mail*].   I
disagree.   None of these cases requires the harsh
outcome reached today.

        . . .   While there are similarities [to *Cox*],
critical aspects of that case make it wholly
distinguishable from this one. First, in [*Cox*], the
victim's name had been disclosed in the hearing where
her assailants pled guilty; and, as we recognized,
judicial records have always been considered public
information in this country. [ ] In fact, even the
earliest notion of privacy rights exempted the
information contained in judicial records from its
protections. [ ] Second, unlike the incident report
at issue here . . . the judicial proceedings at issue
in [*Cox*] were open as a matter of state law. . . .

    These facts . . . were critical to our analysis
in [*Cox*]. . . .

    [*Cox*] stands for the proposition that the State
cannot make the press its first line of defense in
withholding private information from the public--it
cannot ask the press to secrete private facts that the
State makes no effort to safeguard in the first place.
In this case, however, the State has undertaken "means
which avoid [but obviously, not altogether prevent]
public documentation or other exposure of private
information." No doubt this is why the Court frankly
admits that "[*Cox*] . . . cannot fairly be read as
controlling here." [ ]

        . . .

        . . .   I cannot agree that [*Cox, Oklahoma
Publishing, Daily Mail*] require--or even substantially
support--the result reached by the Court today.

                               II

    We are left, then, to wonder whether the three
"independent reasons" the Court cites for reversing
the judgment for B.J.F. support its result. [ ]

The first of these relied on by the Court is the fact "appellant gained access to [B.J.F.'s name] through a government news release." [ ] "The government's issuance of such a release, without qualification, can only convey to recipients that the government considered dissemination lawful," the court suggests. [ ] So described, this case begins to look like the situation in *Oklahoma Publishing*, where a judge invited reporters into his courtroom, but then tried to forbid them from reporting on the proceedings they observed. But this case is profoundly different. Here the "release" of information provided by the government was not, as the Court says, "without qualification." As the Star's own reporter conceded at trial, the crime incident report that inadvertently included B.J.F.'s name was posted in a room that contained signs making it clear that the names of rape victims were not matters of public record, and were not to be published. [ ]   The Star's reporter indicated that she understood that she "[was not] allowed to take down that information" (*i. e.*, B.J.F.'s name) and that "[was] not supposed to take the information from the police department." [ ] Thus, by her own admission the posting of the incident report did not convey to the Star's reporter the idea that "the government considered dissemination lawful"' the Court's suggestion to the contrary is inapt.

Instead, Florida has done precisely what we suggested, in [*Cox*], that States wishing to protect the privacy rights of rape victims might do: "respond [to the challenge] by means which *avoid* public documentation or other exposure of private information." [ ] By amending its public records statute to exempt rape [victims'] names from disclosure, [ ] and forbidding its officials from releasing such information, [ ], the State has taken virtually every step imaginable to prevent what happened here. This case presents a far cry, then, from [*Cox*] or *Oklahoma Publishing*, where the State asked the news media not to publish information it had made generally available to the public: here, the State is not asking the media to do the State's job in the first instance. Unfortunately, as this case illustrates, mistakes happen: even when States take measures to "avoid" disclosure, sometimes rape victim's names are found out. As I see it, it is not too much to ask the press, in instances such as this,

to respect simple standards of decency and refrain
from publishing a victim's name, address, and/or phone
number.

Second, the Court complains that appellant was
judged here under too strict a liability standard.
The Court contends that a newspaper might be found
liable under the Florida courts' negligence *per se*
theory without regard to a newspaper's scienter or
degree of fault.   [ ]   The short answer to this
complaint is that whatever merit the Court's argument
might have, it is totally inapposite here, where the
jury found that appellant acted with "reckless
indifference towards the rights of others," [ ], a
standard far higher than the *Gertz* standard the Court
urges as a constitutional minimum today.   [ ] B.J.F.
proved the Star's negligence at trial--and, actually,
far more than simple negligence; the Court's concerns
about damages resting on a strict liability or mere
causation basis are irrelevant to the validity of the
judgment for appellee.

But even taking the Court's concerns in the
abstract, they miss the mark.   Permitting liability
under a negligence *per se* theory does not mean that
defendants will be held liable without a showing of
negligence, but rather, that the standard of care has
been set by the legislature, instead of the courts.
The Court says that negligence *per se* permits a
plaintiff to hold a defendant liable without a showing
that the disclosure was "of a fact about a person's
private life . . . that a reasonable person would find
highly offensive."   [ ]   But the point here is that
the legislature--reflecting popular sentiment--has
determined that disclosure of the fact that a person
was raped is categorically a revelation that
reasonable people find offensive.   And as for the
Court's suggestion that the Florida courts' theory
permits liability without regard for whether the
victim's identity is already known, or whether she
herself has made it known--these are facts that would
surely enter into the calculation of damages in such
a case.   In any event, none of these mitigating
factors was present here; whatever the force of the
arguments generally, they do not justify the Court's
ruling against B.J.F. in this case.

Third, the Court faults the Florida criminal statute for being underinclusive: § 794.03 covers disclosure of rape [victims'] names in "instrument[s] of mass communication," but not other means of distribution, the Court observes. [ ] But our cases which have struck down laws that limit or burden the press due to their underinclusiveness have involved situations where a legislature has singled out one segment of the news media or press for adverse treatment, [ ]. Here, the Florida law evenhandedly covers all "instrument[s] of mass communication" no matter their form, media, content, nature or purpose. It excludes neighborhood gossips, [ ], because presumably the Florida Legislature has determined that neighborhood gossips do not pose the danger and intrusion to rape victims that "instrument[s] of mass communication" do. Simply put: Florida wanted to prevent the widespread distribution of rape [victims'] names, and therefore enacted a statute tailored almost as precisely as possible to achieving that end.

Moreover, the Court's "underinclusiveness" analysis itself is "underinclusive." After all, the lawsuit against the Star which is at issue here is not an action for violating the statute which the Court deems underinclusive, but is, more accurately, for the negligent publication of appellee's name. [ ] The scheme which the Court should review, then, is not only § 794.03 (which, as noted above, merely provided the standard of care in this litigation), but rather, the whole of Florida privacy tort law. As to the latter, Florida does recognize a tort of publication of private facts. Thus, it is quite possible that the neighborhood gossip whom the Court so fears being left scott-free to spread news of a rape victim's identity would be subjected to the same (or similar) liability regime under which appellant was taxed. The Court's myopic focus on § 794.03 ignores the probability that Florida law is more comprehensive than the Court gives it credit for being.

Consequently, neither the State's "dissemination" of B.J.F.'s name, nor the standard of liability imposed here, nor the underinclusiveness of Florida tort law require setting aside the verdict for B.J.F. And as noted above, such a result is not compelled by our cases. I turn, therefore, to the more general

principles at issue here to see if they recommend the
Court's result.

III

At issue in this case is whether there is any
information about people, which--though true--may not
be published in the press. By holding that only "a
state interest of the highest order" permits the State
to penalize the publication of truthful information,
and by holding that protecting a rape victim's right
to privacy is not among those state interests of the
highest   order,   the   Court   accepts   appellant's
invitation, [ ], to obliterate one of the most note-
worthy legal inventions of the 20th-Century; the tort
of the publication of private facts. [ ] Even if the
Court's opinion does not say as much today, such
obliteration will follow inevitably from the Court's
conclusion here.   If the First Amendment prohibits
wholly   private   persons   (such   as   B.J.F.)   from
recovering from the publication of the fact that she
was raped, I doubt that there remain any "private
facts" which persons may assume will not be published
in the newspapers, or broadcast on television.

Of course, the right to privacy is not absolute.
Even   the   article   widely   relied   upon   in   cases
vindicating privacy rights, Warren & Brandeis, The
Right to Privacy, 4 Harv. L. Rev., at 193, recognized
that this right inevitably conflicts with the public's
right to know about matters of general concern--and
that sometimes, the latter must trump the former. [ ]
Resolving this conflict is a difficult matter, and I
do not fault the Court for attempting to strike an
appropriate balance between the two, but rather, for
according too little weight to B.J.F.'s side of
equation, and too much on the other.

I would strike the balance rather differently.
Writing for the Ninth Circuit, Judge Merrill put this
view eloquently:

"Does the spirit of the Bill of Rights require
that individuals be free to pry into the
unnewsworthy private affairs of their fellowmen?
In our view it does not. In our view, fairly
defined   areas   of   privacy   must   have   the
protection of law if the quality of life is to

continue to be personably acceptable. The public's right to know is, then, subject to reasonable limitations so far as concerns the private facts of its individual members." [ ]

Ironically, this Court, too, had occasion to consider this same balance just a few weeks ago, in *United States Department of Justice v. Reporters Committee for Freedom of the Press*, 489 U.S. 749 [16 Med.L.Rptr. 1545] (1989). There, we were faced with a press request, under the Freedom of Information Act, for a "rap sheet" on a person accused of bribing a Congressman--presumably, a person whose privacy rights would be far less than B.J.F.'s. Yet this Court rejected the media's request for disclosure of the "rap sheet," saying:

"The privacy interest in maintaining the practical obscurity of rap-sheet information will always be high. When the subject of such a rap sheet is a private citizen and when the information is in the Government's control as compilation, rather than as a record of 'what the government is up to,' the privacy interest . . . is . . . at its apex while the . . . public interest in disclosure is at is nadir." [ ]

The Court went on to conclude that disclosure of rap sheets "categorical[ly] constitutes an "unwarranted" invasion of privacy. [ ] The same surely must be true--indeed, much more so--for the disclosure of a rape victim's name.

I do not suggest that the Court's decision today is radical departure from a previously charted course. The Court's ruling has been foreshadowed. In [*Time, Inc. v. Hill*, p. 605 (the casebook, *supra*], we observed that--after a brief period in this century where Brandeis' view was ascendant--the trend in "modern" jurisprudence has been to eclipse an individual's right to maintain private any truthful information that the press wished to publish. More recently, in [*Cox*], we acknowledged the possibility that the First Amendment may prevent a State from ever subjecting the publication of truthful but private information to civil liability. Today, we hit the bottom of the slippery slope.

I would find a place to draw the line higher on the hillside: a spot high enough to protect B.J.F.'s desire for privacy and peace-of-mind in the wake of a horrible personal tragedy. There is no public interest in publishing the names, addresses, and phone numbers of persons who are the victims of crime--and no public interest in immunizing the press from liability in the rare cases where a State's efforts to protect a victim's privacy have failed. Consequently, I respectfully dissent.

Notes and Questions

1. Why is the *Star's* case not precisely covered by *Cox*?

2. Why is the *Star's* case not precisely covered by *Daily Mail*?

3. How might the *Star's* case have been analyzed in a state in which there was no statute?

4. How might the *Star's* case have been analyzed if the *Star* had learned about the name from an eyewitness rather than as the result of a mistake in the sheriff's office?

5. What might change if it turned out that the *Star* got the name from a sheriff's deputy who violated a statute in revealing the name?

6. Does state law or the First Amendment protect a broadcaster that identifies a rape victim in a case in which a man arrested on a rape charge claims that the warden beat him up? (The alleged rape victim is the warden's daughter.) Does *Florida Star* address this?

What analysis in a case in which the rape victim is the daughter of a man who is a strong proponent of criminal rehabilitation and early paroles? What if the rapist had been recently paroled after serving time for rape?

What analysis in a case in which a statute provides that an accused rapist is not to be identified unless and until he is brought to trial?

7.   The decision in *Florida Star* led to a petition seeking review of an earlier case involving an alleged invasion of privacy by a television statement which disclosed the identity of a rape victim.   Ross v. Midwest Communications Inc., 870 F.2d 271, 16 Med.L.Rptr. 1463 (1989).   Marla Ross was raped in 1983 by an assailant who was never apprehended.   Police assured her her name would be held in strict confidence.   In a documentary about the possible innocence of a man accused of another rape, Minneapolis television station WCCO-TV mentioned Ross as "Marla" and showed a photograph of the house in which she lived at the time of the rape.   A federal district court granted summary judgment for the television station, holding that the details of the rape were a matter of legitimate public interest, and the U.S. Court of appeals for the Fifth Circuit affirmed.   In his petition for review following the *Florida Star* case, Ross's attorney told the Supreme Court that its decision in *Florida Star* "shattered the fragile confidence rape survivors possessed in law enforcement promises that their identities would not be disclosed."   Med.L.Rptr. News Notes, Sept. 26, 1989.   The Supreme Court denied certiorari on Oct. 30. 493 U.S. ___ (1989).

8.   In another case, a witness to a murder asserted a privacy claim based on her identification in the *Los Angeles Times* as the person who discovered the body, while the suspect as still at large.   Although there had already been press reports that the body had been found by the "roommate," the California Court of Appeal held that her identity as the discoverer of the body was not yet public and therefore denied summary judgment for the newspaper company.   Times Mirror v. San Diego Superior Court, 244 Cal.Rptr. 556, 198 Cal.App.3d 1420, 15 Med.L.Rptr.1129 (4th Dist.), certiorari dismissed, 109 S.Ct. 1565 (1989).

9.   The highly publicized sexual assault charges against William Kennedy Smith, along with decisions by *The New York Times* and NBC to identify the woman who made the allegations against him, raised anew the concerns about the proper ways of treating complainants in sexual assault cases prior to any court determination that they are, in fact, victims. Public disclosure of the woman's history, particularly in the April 17, 1991, profile of her in the *Times*,

along with public disclosure of other complaints about
Smith, by the prosecutor, led to a postponement of the
trial in August 1991.

Add to casebook p. 633, after last full paragraph:

8.   The "New Kids on the Block" sued *USA Today* and
Star magazine for violating their right of publicity--
along   with   trademark   infringement   and
misappropriation, when the "New Kids" trademark was
used in articles which asked readers to participate,
via a "900" telephone number, in a survey to determine
the group's most popular member.   The U.S. District
Court for the Central District of California held that
the use of the trademark was related to newsgathering
and was not mere commercial exploitation, so the First
Amendment barred the claims. New Kids on the Block v.
News America Publishing, Inc., 745 F.Supp. 1540, 18
Med.L.Rptr. 1089 (C.D.Cal.1990).

9.   *Descendability*. Personal rights such as those
protected by defamation and invasion of privacy law
terminate at death.   Thus, for example, one can
publish   defamatory   statements   about   deceased
individuals with impunity (unless the same statement
also defames people who are still alive). Because the
right of publicity is a property right, a great
controversy has developed as to whether it survives
the death of its creator.

        Currently,   there   seem   to   be   three   distinct
approaches being taken by various courts. One is that
the right terminates upon death. Under this view, as
soon as people die, their names, likenesses and
characterizations are available for anyone to use
without legal liability. At the other extreme is the
position that death has no effect on the right of
publicity. In jurisdictions adhering to this view,
the consent of whoever owns the property in question
(perhaps the individual's heirs or someone who has
purchased the right) is always necessary. Finally,
there is an intermediate approach that holds the right
of publicity to survive death only if it was
commercially exploited during the person's lifetime.

        If the right of publicity continues beyond death
(either because it always does or because it was

commercially exploited during the person's lifetime), the next question is how long it lasts.   A state statute might stipulate a specific number of years, or the right of publicity might last as long as it continues to be exploited by the individual's heirs or forever.   State statutes that provide for survivability do so for varying periods of time ranging from 10 years after death in Tennessee to 50 years after death in California.

Chapter XIV

SPECIAL PROBLEMS OF ELECTRONIC MEDIA JOURNALISTS

Add to casebook p. 635, after 2nd full paragraph:

The outbreak of war in the Persian Gulf in January 1991 led to two major issues in government-press relations which are always present in wartime. One is access by the journalists to the people they want to interview and the places they want to go to cover stories. The other issue is direct censorship by the government of journalists' reports from the war area--something that would clearly be intolerable in peacetime and is viewed by some as equally intolerable in wartime. The separation between the two issues is not always distinct: sometimes government may give journalists access to a place only on the condition that they submit their reports for review. In those instances the journalists are, in a sense, consenting to being censored; but it may be the only way they can get to the sources of the news.

By early February 1991, there were more than 500 journalists covering the war, and there were already complaints about censorship. Despite general agreement about the need to respect military secrecy about the location and numbers of troops and about specific military plans and strategies, there were inevitable disagreements about what needed to be secret and what did not. There were complaints by journalists that the military personnel assigned to review their stories were unqualified or were simply slow.

Malcolm W. Browne of *The New York Times* said that there had been instances in which information censored by military officials at the scene was later released in Washington. He also pointed out that print reporters had to submit written texts for review, but broadcasters often reported live--and therefore without review. "Where's the Beef?," Editor & Publisher, Jan. 26, 1991 at 9.

Paul McMasters, national Freedom of Information chairman for the Society of Professional Journalists, said, "To me, it's still obvious that there are too many restrictions on reporting. . . . The tide is eventually going to turn. The public is starting to express unease with the almost total control of information." Burl Osborne, president of the American Society of Newspaper Editors, in a letter to the Department of Defense, said, "We recognize, as a predicate, that security ought to be paramount in your considerations. Reporters have demonstrated in the past that they will abide by reasonable security guidelines. . . . The experience of the last two weeks tends to confirm that, even in this new environment of instant communications capability, journalists recognize the need to maintain military security." he recommended throwing out the prior review requirement. "Press Pools on the Verge of Collapse?," Editor & Publisher, Feb. 2, 1991 at 7.

Add to casebook p. 638, after 2nd full paragraph:

In June 1991 the Supreme Court of the United States reversed a judgment against Attorney Dominic P. Gentile, who had held a press conference the day after his client was indicted on criminal charges. The client was acquitted by a jury six months later, and the Disciplinary Board of the State Bar of Nevada subsequently found that Gentile had violated a Nevada Supreme Court Rule prohibiting lawyers from making extrajudicial statements to the press that they know or reasonably should know would have a "substantial likelihood of materially prejudicing" a proceeding. The Nevada Supreme Court had affirmed, rejecting Gentile's contention that the rule violated his right to free speech.

The Supreme Court of the United States reversed, holding that the "substantial likelihood of material prejudice" test applied by Nevada and most other states satisfies the First Amendment but that the Nevada rule was nonetheless void for vagueness: its grammatical structure and the absence of clarifying interpretation failed to provide fair notice to lawyers. Gentile v. State Bar of Nevada, 501 U.S. ____, 111 S.Ct. 2720 (1991).

Add to casebook p. 642, after 2nd full paragraph:

Recall *Noriega* (from Chapter I, this Supplement), in which a temporary restraint was imposed on CNN to stop the network from broadcasting taperecorded telephone calls between Noriega and members of his defense team.

Add to casebook p. 642, after 3rd full paragraph:

Gags on Grand Jurors. In another attempt to cut off information at its source, a Florida law prohibited grand jury witnesses from disclosing their testimony. When a journalist was himself a grand jury witness, the statute effectively became a restraint on publication. In a 1990 case, the Supreme Court found the statute to violate the First Amendment. Michael Smith, a reporter for the *Charlotte Herald-News* in Charlotte County, Fla., had been called to testify before a special grand jury about information he had obtained while writing a series of newspaper stories about alleged improprieties committed by the Charlotte County state attorney's office and sheriff's department. He had been warned that any disclosure of his testimony would violate the Florida statute. Writing for a unanimous court, Chief Justice Rehnquist acknowledged various state interests in keeping grand jury testimony secret but concluded that they were insufficient "to overcome [Smith's] First Amendment right to make a truthful statement of the information he had acquired on his own." Butterworth v. Smith, 17 Med.L.Rptr. 1569 (1990).

Add to casebook p. 650, after 2nd full paragraph:

The New York State experiment was continued in a second phase which ended May 31, 1991, with state legislators unable to agree to terms of a third phase of the experiment. It will be autumn before lawmakers will have another opportunity to pass legislation allowing cameras to return to New York trial courts. Med.L.Rptr., News Notes, June 11, 1991.

A three-year experiment with photographic and electronic media coverage of civil proceedings in federal courts began July 1, 1991, and is scheduled to end June 30, 1994. Approval of the experiment by the U.S. Judicial Conference was for two federal appeals courts and up to six federal district courts. The circuit courts chosen were the U.S. Circuit Courts of Appeals in New York (2nd Circuit) and San Francisco (9th Circuit). The district courts chosen were those in the Southern District of New York (New York City), the Western District of Washington (Seattle), the Eastern District of Pennsylvania (Philadelphia), the District of Massachusetts (Boston), the Eastern District of Michigan (Detroit, Ann Arbor, Bay City, Flint and Fort Huron), and the Southern District of Indiana (Indianapolis, Evansville, Muncie, New Albany and Terre Haute).

Add to casebook p. 660, after 1st partial paragraph:

New York State's shield law was amended in March 1990 to provide a qualified exemption from contempt charges for journalists who fail to disclose non-confidential news sources. Journalists in the state had pressed for the change following controversy over a television station was asked to provide tapes of an interview with a murder suspect that was taped before the subject became a suspect and with no promise of confidentiality. Med.L.Rptr. News Notes, April 3, 1990.

The Florida Supreme Court held that journalists in that state have no privilege to protect them against testifying in a court proceeding as to their eyewitness observations of a relevant event. The Miami Herald Publishing Co. v. Morejon, Med.L.Rptr. News Notes, June 12, 1990.

Add to casebook p. 668, after 1st partial paragraph:

The Minnesota Supreme Court, in a 4-to-2 decision, overturned the decision in July 1990. The court held that Cohen and the reporters had not intended to create a contract when they negotiated the terms under which Cohen sought and was promised confidentiality. The majority opinion said, "Contract law seems here an ill fit for a promise of news source confidentiality." New York Times, July 21, 1990, at p. A-6.

The Supreme Court of the United States decided the case almost a year later:

COHEN V. COWLES MEDIA COMPANY
Supreme Court of the United States
501 U.S. ____, 111 S.Ct. 2513,
18 Med.L.Rptr. 2273 (1991)

JUSTICE WHITE delivered the opinion of the Court.

The question before us is whether the First Amendment prohibits a plaintiff from recovering damages, under state promissory estoppel law, for a newspaper's breach of a promise of confidentiality given to the plaintiff in exchange for information. We hold that it does not.

During the closing days of the 1982 Minnesota gubernatorial race, Dan Cohen, an active Republican associated with Wheelock Whitney's Independent-Republican gubernatorial campaign, approached reporters from the St. Paul Pioneer Press Dispatch (Pioneer Press) and the Minneapolis Star and Tribune (Star Tribune) and offered to provide documents relating to a candidate in the upcoming election. Cohen made clear to the reporters that he would provide the information only if he was given a promise of confidentiality. Reporters from both papers promised to keep Cohen's identity anonymous and Cohen turned over copies of two public court records concerning Marlene Johnson, the Democratic-Farmer-Labor candidate for Lieutenant Governor. The first record indicated that Johnson had been charged in 1969 with three counts of unlawful assembly, and the second that she had been convicted in 1970 of petit theft. Both newspapers interviewed Johnson for her explanation and one reporter tracked down the person who had found the records for Cohen. As it turned out, the unlawful assembly charges arose out of Johnson's participation in a protest of an alleged failure to hire minority workers on municipal construction projects and the charges were eventually dismissed. The petit theft conviction was for leaving a store without paying for $6.00 worth of sewing materials. The incident apparently occurred at a time during which Johnson was emotionally distraught, and the conviction was later vacated.

After consultation and debate, the editorial staffs of the two newspapers independently decided to publish Cohen's name as part of their stories concerning Johnson. In their stories, both papers identified Cohen as the source of the court records, indicated his connection to the Whitney campaign, and included denials by Whitney campaign officials of any role in the matter. The same day the stories appeared, Cohen was fired by his employer.

Cohen sued respondents, the publishers of the Pioneer Press and Star Tribune, in Minnesota state court, alleging fraudulent misrepresentation and breach of contract. The trial court rejected respondents' argument that the First Amendment barred Cohen's lawsuit. A jury returned a verdict in Cohen's favor, awarding him $200,000 in compensatory damages and $500,000 in punitive damages. The Minnesota Court of Appeals, in a split decision, reversed the award of punitive damages after concluding that Cohen had failed to establish a fraud claim, the only claim which would support such an award. 445 N.W. 2d 248, 260 (Minn. App. 1989). However, the court upheld the finding of liability for breach of contract and the $200,000 compensatory damage award. Id., at 262.

A divided Minnesota Supreme Court reversed the compensatory damages award. [ ] After affirming the Court of Appeals' determination that Cohen had not established a claim for fraudulent misrepresentation, the court considered his breach of contract claim and concluded that "a contract cause of action is inappropriate for these particular circumstances." [ ] The court then went on to address the question whether Cohen could establish a cause of action under Minnesota law on a promissory estoppel theory. Apparently, a promissory estoppel theory was never tried to the jury, nor briefed, nor argued by the parties; it first arose during oral argument in the Minnesota Supreme Court when one of the justices asked a question about equitable estoppel. [ ]

In addressing the promissory estoppel question, the court decided that the most problematic element in establishing such a cause of action here was whether injustice could be avoided only by enforcing the promise of confidentiality made to Cohen. The court stated the "[u]nder a promissory estoppel analysis there can be no neutrality towards the First Amendment. In deciding whether it would be unjust not to enforce the promise, the court must necessarily weigh the same considerations that are weighed for whether the First Amendment has been violated. The court must balance the interest in protecting a promise of anonymity." [ ] After a brief discussion, the court concluded that "in this case enforcement of the promise of confidentiality under a promissory estoppel theory would violate defendants' First Amendment rights." [ ]

We granted certiorari to consider the First Amendment implications of this case. [ ]

Respondents initially contend that the Court should dismiss this case without reaching the merits because the promissory estoppel theory was not argued or presented in the courts below and because the Minnesota Supreme Court's decision rests entirely on the interpretation of state law. These contentions do not merit extended discussion. It is irrelevant to this Court's jurisdiction whether a party raised below and argued a federal-law issue that the state supreme court actually considered and decided. [ ] Moreover, that the Minnesota Supreme Court rested its holding on federal law could not be made more clear than by its conclusion that "in this case enforcement of the promise of confidentiality under a promissory estoppel theory would violate defendants' First Amendment rights." [ ] It can hardly be said that there is no First Amendment issue present in the case when respondents have defended against this suit all along by arguing that the First Amendment barred the enforcement of the reporters' promises to Cohen. We proceed to consider whether that Amendment bars a promissory estoppel cause of action against respondents.

The initial question we face is whether a private cause of action for promissory estoppel involves "state action" within the meaning of the Fourteenth Amendment such that the protections of the First Amendment are triggered. For if it does not, then the First Amendment has no bearing on this case. The rationale of our decision in [*New York Times Co. v. Sullivan*, p. 539 (the casebook), *supra*], and subsequent cases compels the conclusion that there is state action here.   Our cases teach that the application of state rules of law in state courts in a manner alleged to restrict First Amendment freedoms constitutes "state action" under the Fourteenth Amendment. [ ] In this case, the Minnesota Supreme Court held that if Cohen could recover at all it would be on the theory of promissory estoppel, a state-law doctrine which, in the absence of a contract, creates obligations never explicitly assumed by the parties. These legal obligations would be enforced through the official power of the Minnesota courts.   Under our cases, that is enough to constitute "state action" for purposes of the Fourteenth Amendment.

Respondents rely on the proposition that "if a newspaper lawfully obtains truthful information about a matter of public significance then state officials may not constitutionally punish publication of the information, absent a need to further a state interest of the highest order."   [*Smith v. Daily Mail Publishing Co.*, p. 27 (the casebook), *supra*].   That proposition is unexceptionable, and it has been applied in various cases that have found insufficient the asserted state interests in preventing publication of truthful, lawfully obtained information. [ ]

This case however, is not controlled by this line of cases but rather by the equally well-established line of decisions holding that generally applicable laws do not offend the First Amendment simply because their enforcement against the press has incidental effects on its ability to gather and report the news. As the cases relied on by respondents recognize, the truthful information sought to be published must have been lawfully acquired.   The press may not with impunity break and enter an office or dwelling to gather news. Neither does the First Amendment relieve a newspaper reporter of the obligation shared by all citizens to respond to a grand jury subpoena and answer questions relevant to a criminal investigation, even though the reporter might be required to reveal a confidential source.   [*Branzburg*, p. 656 (the casebook), *supra*]. The press, like others interested in publishing, may not publish copyrighted material without obeying the copyright laws. See [*Zacchini*, p. 626 (the casebook), *supra*]. Similarly, the media must obey the National Labor Relations Act, [ ], and the Fair Labor Standards Act, [ ]; may not restrain trade in violation of the antitrust laws [ ]; and must pay nondiscriminatory taxes. [ ] It is therefore beyond dispute that "[t]he publisher of a newspaper has no special immunity from the application of general laws. He has no special privilege to invade the rights and liberties of others." [ ] Accordingly, enforcement of such general laws against the press is not subject to stricter scrutiny than would be applied to enforcement against other persons or organizations.

There can be little doubt that the Minnesota doctrine of promissory estoppel is a law of general applicability. It does not target or single out the press. Rather, in so far as we are advised, the doctrine is generally applicable to the daily transactions of all the citizens of Minnesota.

Justice Blackmun suggests that applying Minnesota promissory estoppel doctrine in this case will "punish" Respondents for publishing truthful information that was lawfully obtained. [ ] This is not strictly accurate because compensatory damages are not a form of punishment, as were the criminal sanctions at issue in Smith. If the contract between the parties in this case had contained a liquidated damages provision, it would be perfectly clear that the payment to petitioner would represent a cost of acquiring newsworthy material to be published at a profit, rather than a punishment imposed by the State. The payment of compensatory damages in this case is constitutionally indistinguishable from a generous bonus paid to a confidential news source. In any event, as indicated above, the characterization of the payment makes no difference for First Amendment purposes when the law being applied is a general law and does not single out the press. Moreover, Justice Blackmun's reliance on cases like [The Florida Star and Smith] is misplaced. In those cases, the State itself defined the content of publications that would trigger liability. Here, by contrast, Minnesota law simply requires those making promises to keep them. The parties themselves, as in this case, determine the scope of their legal obligations and any restrictions which may be placed on the publication of truthful information are self-imposed.

Also, it is not at all clear that Respondents obtained Cohen's name "lawfully" in this case, at least for purposes of publishing it.   Unlike the situation in *The Florida Star*, where the rape victim's name was obtained through lawful access to a police report, respondents obtained Cohen's name only by making a promise which they did not honor.   The dissenting opinions suggest that the press should not be subject to any law, including copyright law for example, which in any fashion or to any degree limits or restricts the press' right to report truthful information.   The First Amendment does not grant the press such limitless protection.

Nor is Cohen attempting to use a promissory estoppel cause of action to avoid the strict requirements for establishing a libel or defamation claim.   As the Minnesota Supreme Court observed here, "Cohen could not sue for defamation because the information disclosed [his name] was true."   [ ] Cohen is not seeking damages for injury to his reputation or his state of mind. He sought damages in excess of $50,000 for breach of a promise that caused him to lose his job and lowered his earning capacity. Thus this is not a case like [*Hustler*, p. 571 (the casebook), *supra*, where we held that the constitutional libel standards apply to a claim alleging that the publication of a parody was a state-law tort of intentional infliction of emotional distress.

Respondents and amici argue that permitting Cohen to maintain a cause of action for promissory estoppel will inhibit truthful reporting because news organizations will have legal incentives not to disclose a confidential source's identity even when that person's identity is itself newsworthy. Justice Souter makes a similar argument.   But if this is the case, it is no more than the incidental, and constitutionally insignificant, consequence of applying to the press a generally applicable law that requires those who make certain kinds of promises to keep them.   Although we conclude that the First does not confer on the press a constitutional right to disregard promises that would otherwise be enforced under state law, we reject Cohen's request that in reversing the Minnesota Supreme Court's judgment we reinstate the jury verdict awarding him $200,000 in compensatory damages.   [ ] The Minnesota Supreme Court's incorrect conclusion that the First Amendment barred Cohen's claim may well have truncated its consideration of whether a promissory estoppel claim had otherwise been established under Minnesota law and whether Cohen's jury verdict could be upheld on a promissory estoppel basis. Or perhaps the State Constitution may be construed to shield the press from a promissory estoppel cause of action such as this one. These are matters for the Minnesota Supreme Court to address and resolve in the first instance on remand. Accordingly, the judgment of the Minnesota Supreme Court is reversed, and the case is remanded for further proceedings not inconsistent with this opinion.

So ordered.

Justice Blackmun, with whom Justice Marshall and Justice Souter join, dissenting.

. . .

Contrary to the majority, I regard our decision in [Hustler] to be precisely on point. There, we found that the use of a claim of intentional infliction of emotional distress to impose liability for the publication of a satirical critique violated the First Amendment. There was no doubt that Virginia's tort of intentional infliction of emotional distress was "a law of general applicability" unrelated to the suppression of speech. Nonetheless, a unanimous Court found that, when used to penalize the expression of opinion, the law was subject to the strictures of the First Amendment. In applying that principle, we concluded, [ ], that "public figures and public officials may not recover for the tort of intentional infliction of emotional distress by reason of publications such as the one here at issue without showing in addition that the publication contains a false statement of fact which was made with 'actual malice.'" as defined by [Sullivan]. In so doing, we rejected the argument that Virginia's interest in protecting its citizens from emotional distress was sufficient to remove from First Amendment protection a "patently offensive" expression of opinion. [*Hustler*][3]

As in *Hustler*, the operation of Minnesota's doctrine of promissory estoppel in this case cannot be said to have a merely "incidental" burden on speech; the publication of important political speech is the claimed violation. Thus, as in *Hustler*, the law may not be enforced to punish the expression of truthful information or opinion.[4] In the instant case, it is undisputed that the publication at issue was true.

To the extent that truthful speech may ever be sanctioned consistent with the First Amendment, it must be in furtherance of a state interest "of the highest order." [*Smith*]. Because the Minnesota Supreme Court's opinion makes clear that the State's interest in enforcing its promissory estoppel doctrine in this case was far from compelling, [ ], I would affirm that court's decision.

---

[3] The majority attempts to distinguish *Hustler* on the ground that there the plaintiff sought damages for injury to his state of mind whereas the petitioner here sought damages "for a breach of a promise that caused him to lose his job and lowered his earning capacity." [ ] I perceive no meaningful distinction between a statute that penalizes published speech in order to protect the individual's psychological well being or reputational interest, and one that exacts the same penalty in order to compensate the loss of employment or earning potential. Certainly, our decision in *Hustler* recognized no such distinction.

[4] The majority argues that, unlike the criminal sanctions we considered in [*Smith*,] the liability at issue here will not "punish" respondents in the strict sense of that word. [ ] While this may be true, we have long held that the imposition of civil liability based on protected expression constitutes "punishment" of speech for First Amendment purposes. See, e.g., [*Pittsburgh Press, Gertz*]. Though they be civil, the sanctions we review in this case are no more justifiable as "a cost of acquiring newsworthy material," [ ], than were the libel damages at issue in *New York Times* a permissible cost of disseminating newsworthy material.

I respectfully dissent.

JUSTICE SOUTER, with whom JUSTICE MARSHALL, JUSTICE BLACKMUN and JUSTICE O'CONNOR join, dissenting.

I agree with Justice Blackmun that this case does not fall within the line of authority holding the press to laws of general applicability where commercial activities and relationships, not the content of publication, are at issue. . . . "There is nothing talismanic about natural laws of general applicability," [ ] for such laws may restrict First Amendment rights just as effectively as those directed specifically at speech itself.   Because I do not believe the fact of general applicability to be dispositive, I find it necessary to articulate, measure, and compare the competing interests involved in any given case to determine the legitimacy of burdening constitutional interests, and such has been the Court's recent practice in publication cases. [ ]

Nor can I accept the majority's position that we may dispense with balancing because the burden on publication is in a sense "self-imposed" by the newspaper's voluntary promise of confidentiality. [ ] This suggests both the possibility of waiver, the requirements for which have not been met here [see *Curtis Publishing Co.*], as well as a conception of First Amendment rights as those of the speaker alone, with a value that may be measured without reference to the importance of the information to public discourse. But freedom of the press is ultimately founded on the value of enhancing such discourse for the sake of a citizenry better informed and thus more prudently self-governed." . . .

The importance of this public interest is integral to the balance that should be struck in this case.   There can be no doubt that the fact of Cohen's identity expanded the universe of information relevant to the choice faced by Minnesota voters in that State's 1982 gubernatorial election, the publication of which was thus of the sort quintessentially subject to strict First Amendment protection.   [ ]   The propriety of his leak to respondents could be taken to reflect on his character, which in turn could be taken to reflect on the character of the candidate who had retained him as an adviser.   An election could turn on just such a factor; if it should, I am ready to assume that it would be to the greater public good, at least over the long run.

This is not to say that the breach of such a promise of confidentiality could never give rise to liability. One can conceive of situations in which the injured party is a private individual, whose identity is of less public concern than that of the petitioner; liability there might not be constitutionally prohibited. Nor do I mean to imply that the circumstances of acquisition are irrelevant to the balance, see, e.g., [*Florida Star*], although they may go only to what balances against, and not to diminish, the First Amendment value of any particular piece of information.

Because I believe the State's interest in enforcing a newspaper's promise of confidentiality insufficient to outweigh the interest in unfettered publication of the information revealed in this case, I respectfully dissent.

Notes and Questions

1.   Note that the decision leaves the Minnesota Supreme Court free to decide that the potential interference with editorial autonomy, which it mistakenly thought would violate the First Amendment, does violate state policies underlying the equitable remedy of promissory estoppel. Should the state court have decided the case on that basis in the first instance?

The newspapers argued that the state court decision in fact rested on such a ground, and that the Supreme Court therefore lacked jurisdiction. The Supreme Court rejected the argument, noting that the state court had concluded that "in this case enforcement of the promise of confidentiality under a promissory estoppel theory would violate defendants' First Amendment rights." If the state court had substituted "free speech rights" for the last three words, would its decision have been reviewable by the Supreme Court?

2.   Newspapers and other media often enter into contracts that restrict the dissemination of news.

For example, some newspapers operate news services through which they make their reports available to other newspapers subject to many conditions, including payment of fees and observance of release times and publication dates. Networks make their programs, including news programs, available to affiliates under contracts that impose similar conditions. If an affiliate or a subscribing newspaper insisted on a constitutional right to publish without complying with those conditions, how would the dissenters distinguish that case from *Cohen*?

3. The majority opinion does not respond to Justice Blackmun's argument that the burden on speech arising from liability for breach of a promise is no more "incidental" than the burden arising from libel or intentional infliction of emotional distress. Is there a satisfactory answer to that argument? If all civil liability for publication were treated as imposing similar burdens on speech, what constitutional limitations on contract liability might be suggested by the libel analogy?

4. In the reporter's privilege cases, media argue that unless they are allowed to honor promises of confidentiality, sources will not be willing to rely on those promises and will stop communicating to reporters, thereby chilling the flow of information to the public. Would a similar chilling effect occur if courts held that promises of confidentiality were not enforceable?

Add to casebook p. 670, at end of page:

Texas newspaper reporter Brian Karem spent 14 days in jail after he refused to disclose the names of confidential sources who assisted him in obtaining a jail house telephone interview with an accused murderer. Karem had been sentenced to six months in jail and fined $500 for contempt, but he was released when his source allowed her identity to be revealed. Jane Kirtley of the Reporters Committee for Freedom of the Press said it was the first time in more than 10 years that a journalist had had to spend more than a few days in jail for refusing to reveal confidential information. Med.L.Rptr. News Notes July 17, 1990.

Add to casebook p. 675, after note 7:

8.   The Supreme Court of the United States held in March 1989 that third party requests for law enforcement records or information about a private citizen (even one charged with or convicted of a crime) "can reasonably be expected to invade that citizen's privacy," and that the FBI's criminal identification or "rap sheet" records are therefore exempt from disclosure under the Freedom of Information Act.   Justice Department v. Reporters Committee for Freedom of the Press, 489 U.S. 749, 109 S.Ct. 1468, 16 Med.L.Rptr. 1545 (1989).

9.   The widespread use of computers for information storage presents quite different problems for requestors of information than existed when the Freedom of Information Act was passed.   Receiving a computer tape of government data will do requestors little good if they do not have the computer software necessary to access the data.   Government sometimes argues, however, that the purchase agreements it made when it purchased computer software do not permit it to give free copies of the software to parties who are requesting the data.   It has also been alleged that there are instances in which government has switched from one computer program to another, archived the old records, and then failed to save the software necessary to access the data in its own archives-- essentially rendering the data useless for government as well as for requestors.   The Reporters Committee for Freedom of the Press issued a 30-page booklet about access to electronic records in August 1990.

Add to casebook p. 681 after 5th full paragraph:

When U.S. troops were sent to Saudi Arabia in August 1990 following Iraq's invasion of Kuwait, the complaints about the pool arrangements surfaced again. Two pools were called nearly a week after the first U.S. troops arrived. One went to Saudi Arabia and the other pool members were sent to U.S. Navy ships in the area.   The Secretary of Defense attributed the delay in sending the pools to Saudi objections to the media presence.   Editor & Publisher, Aug. 18, 1990 at 11.

In the months leading up to the start of the air war in January 1991, the Pentagon came up with new regulations for combat pool reporters, including a requirement that the reporters pass a physical fitness test involving push-ups, sit-ups and a mile-and-a-half run. Requirements were adjusted according to age and sex, and reportedly few journalists had trouble with them. Editor & Publisher, Jan. 12, 1991 at 8. During the air war in January and February there were numerous press complaints about required "security review" of their stories and about allegations that their military escorts took them to unnewsworthy locations and sometimes picked the soldiers to be interviewed. There were also complaints that pool reports--particularly reports by print media reporters--sometimes took hours to be reviewed, even though broadcast journalists sometimes were able to send live transmissions with little or no interference from their military escorts. Even before the outbreak of hostilities, nine publications and four journalists brought suit against the Department of Defense charging unfair practices and seeking an injunction against implementing the press policies. The suit was filed by the New York-based Center for Constitutional Rights. Broadcasting, "Journalists in a War of Strict Press Rules," Jan. 28, 1991 at 22.

Press concerns over problems in war coverage continued long after the war ended. Seventeen leaders of U.S. media sent Secretary of Defense Dick Cheney a letter and report describing the Gulf war as "the most under-covered major conflict in modern American history." They said they believed "the Pentagon pool arrangements during Operation Desert Storm made it impossible for reporters and photographers to tell the public the full story of the war in a timely fashion." Editor & Publisher, July 6, 1991 at 7.

Notes

Notes

Notes

Notes